CONVERSATIONS WITH
RBG

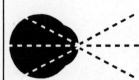
This Large Print Book carries the
Seal of Approval of N.A.V.H.

CONVERSATIONS WITH RBG

RUTH BADER GINSBURG ON LIFE, LOVE, LIBERTY, AND LAW

JEFFREY ROSEN

THORNDIKE PRESS
A part of Gale, a Cengage Company

LIBRARY OF CONGRESS CIP DATA ON FILE.
CATALOGUING IN PUBLICATION FOR THIS BOOK
IS AVAILABLE FROM THE LIBRARY OF CONGRESS

ISBN-13: 978-1-4328-7828-3 (hardcover alk. paper)

Published in 2020 by arrangement with Henry Holt and Company

Printed in Mexico
Print Number: 03   Print Year: 2020

For my beloved mother,
Estelle Rosen
April 8, 1933–January 27, 2019

"Even when one is all grown up, death of a beloved parent is a loss difficult to bear. But you will honor your mother best if you carry on with your work and days, thriving in the challenges and joys of being alive. Isn't that just what she would have willed?"

— JUSTICE RUTH BADER GINSBURG

CONTENTS

INTRODUCTION 9

1. Her Landmark Cases 31
2. Marriage Between Equals 51
3. *Roe* 70
4. The Bill of Rights and Equal
   Protection 90
5. Sisters in Law 115
6. Nino 138
7. The Two Chiefs 153
8. When a Dissent Sparked a
   Meme 167
9. The Cases She Would Overturn . . 192
10. Measured Motions 212
11. #MeToo and a More Perfect
    Union 232
12. Margaret Atwood Meets RBG . . 256
13. The Heroic Legacy 273

NOTES 293
ACKNOWLEDGMENTS 311

INTRODUCTION

One of the luckiest relationships of my life began with a chance encounter in an elevator. I first met Ruth Bader Ginsburg in 1991, when I was a young law clerk on the U.S. Court of Appeals for the District of Columbia Circuit. She was a judge on the same court, and I ran into her as she was on her way back from a workout class called "Jazzercize." She was a formidable presence, and as we rode the elevator, she maintained the sphinxlike silence that those who don't know her can mistake for remoteness.

To break the ice, and unable to think of anything else to say, I asked her which operas she had seen recently. I don't think I knew she was an opera fan, but it seemed like a safe topic. We bonded immediately over our mutual love of opera and began a conversation about music that has continued ever since.

A year later, I was hired to be the legal affairs editor of the *New Republic.* This was another lucky break: at the age of twenty-eight, I had fallen into my dream job, writing about the law and the Supreme Court for a Washington magazine whose legal writers had included constitutional legends such as Learned Hand, Felix Frankfurter, and Alexander Bickel. Ginsburg and I began corresponding about my first *New Republic* articles and about the latest operas she had seen. When I sent her a piece after the 1992 presidential election arguing that Justice Antonin Scalia had become the "Leader of the Opposition" to an incoming Democratic president and Congress, she replied diplomatically, "Interesting article about my friend, the Justice." A few weeks later, on January 21, 1993, in response to an article about a lackluster performance of *Otello* at the Washington National Opera, she wrote:

Hope you and a friend are free to attend the Wednesday, February 17 *Turandot* rehearsal. No forecast about the performance, but seats are up front on the aisle . . . The other opera this fall was the *Tsar's Bride.* I wish you had attended that one instead of *Otello.* It might have prompted kinder thoughts about the Washington opera.

After I attended the *Turandot* rehearsal and thanked her for the tickets, she saw the opening performance and shared her thoughts in a letter dated February 25: "*Turandot* was grand opera. The chorus, especially in the first act, was spectacular in the performance I attended last night. Diva Eva sang in a very full voice and the Calaf did a better job than I expected with "Nessun Dorma." Glad you had a chance to see the local company in brighter light and more comfortable seats."

In the same letter, she also responded to an article I'd sent praising Justice David H. Souter but criticizing the "cult of Harlan" that had developed around the justice he had invoked as his hero, Justice John Marshall Harlan II, a moderate conservative justice from the Warren era whom both liberals and conservatives on the Court were embracing as a model of judicial restraint.

Enjoyed your comment on Justice Souter, but think you give Justice Harlan less credit than he merits. Gerry Gunther, my dear teacher and friend, has the highest regard for Harlan, because he almost always gave us a full accounting for his position, without guise or fanfare. A typical example is his concurring opinion in *Welsh v. United States,* which proved a great aid to me in my equal rights advocacy days.

Ginsburg's citation of the *Welsh* case, from 1970, showed her strategic vision as an advocate as well as her respect for Harlan's transparency as a judge. In that opinion, Harlan had held that the remedy for a constitutional violation is either extension or invalidation: in other words, if a court concludes that a law violates the Constitution by discriminating in favor of a particular group, it can either invalidate the discriminatory law in question or extend its benefits to the excluded class. Ginsburg invoked Harlan's opinion in *Welsh* in a 1979 law review article called "Some Thoughts on Judicial Authority to Repair Unconstitutional Legislation," where she explained that the *Welsh* opinion had inspired her as an advocate to ask the Supreme Court to extend Social Security and public assistance benefits to both men and women in cases where one or the other gender had been excluded because of discriminatory stereotypes.[1] The *Welsh* case also informed her strategy in the first gender equality case she won, *Moritz v. Commissioner of Internal Revenue,* now immortalized in the 2018 movie *On the Basis of Sex.*

In *Moritz,* she successfully persuaded a federal appellate court to extend a tax benefit that had previously been available only to single women who cared for their dependent parents to single men in the same situation.

Emboldened by this friendly correspondence, I sent Judge Ginsburg flowers for her sixtieth birthday on March 15 and she responded three days later with a handwritten card: "The flowers now brighten the first sitting of my 60s and will help me think of spring this weekend." She added that she had just seen a dress rehearsal for Janacek's *Cunning Little Vixen:* "Three puntas to me for not asking you to join my chambers team for the *Vixen* Look-In Washington Opera did March 10 at noon. With appreciation, RBG."

On March 20, Justice Byron R. White retired from the Supreme Court. Ginsburg was one of several candidates being considered to replace him, but her nomination was opposed by some women's groups who viewed her as insufficiently liberal because she had criticized the legal reasoning in the Court's landmark abortion rights decision, *Roe v. Wade.*

In late April I wrote a piece for the *New Republic* called "The List," ranking the seven leading candidates in ascending order and concluding with Ginsburg. "Of all the candidates" on President Bill Clinton's short list, I wrote, "Ginsburg is the most respected both by liberals and conservatives.

> Her scrupulous position on *Roe* represents Clinton's best opportunity to cut the Gordian knot of the litmus test; and she is the candidate most likely to win over the swing justices in memos and at conference. The only concern about Ginsburg is that she might become too friendly with the mushy middle. But although she has been willing to compromise on minor details, her core positions — on broad access to the courts, freedom of religion and speech and gender equality — are models of principled liberalism. Her nomination would be one of the most acclaimed since Felix Frankfurter, who turned Ginsburg down for a clerkship in 1960 on the grounds that he wasn't ready for a woman. Now, we are.[2]

A few weeks earlier, although I didn't know it at the time, Marty Ginsburg, the judge's husband, had begun a quiet campaign to convince Senator Daniel Patrick Moynihan of New York to champion her nomination. (Moynihan, initially skeptical, came to relish the chance to take on his colleague Senator Edward Kennedy of Massachusetts, who was supporting the candidacy of a hometown federal appeals court judge, Stephen G. Breyer, who sat in Boston.) "I surely saw your editorials and had them in mind when I first spoke to the President," Moynihan wrote to me on June 21, 1993. "On the other hand, there appears no question that by the beginning of the week of June 8th, the President had narrowed the choices down to three candidates: Judge Breyer, Judge [Gilbert] Merritt, and Secretary [of the Interior Bruce] Babbitt. Then, of a sudden, Judge Ginsburg reappeared."

Moynihan later wrote an unpublished letter faxed to the *New Republic* about his role in what came next.

On May 12, 1993, I was flying to New York with the President along with [his aides] Harold Ickes and David Wilhelm. Two-thirds of the way up, he puts aside his speech, turns to me, and says, who should I nominate for the Supreme Court? I say, there is surely only one name, Ruth Bader Ginsburg. He says, the women are against her. I say, that is yet another reason. They are mad about her Madison lecture at NYU [where she had criticized the reasoning in *Roe v. Wade*]. But surely she was right. End subject.

One month later, on June 11, I call [White House communications director David] Gergen about something or another and pretty much as an afterthought, he asks who I would like to see on the Court. I relate my exchange with the President. In the meantime, I have received a copy of a letter to the President from Michael Sovern, then President of Columbia, in which he mentioned a talk that Dean Erwin Griswold gave at the Court on the occasion of the 50th anniversary of their moving into the new building. Dean Griswold mentioned various members of the Supreme Court bar active in this period. He particularly noted Thurgood Marshall in the area of racial equality and Ruth Bader Ginsburg in the area of gender equality. Gergen asks if I could send him that talk. It happened that my assistant, Eleanor Suntum, has a sister who worked at the Court and had worked in its library. Without my knowing, Eleanor called her sister and the text was faxed over within the hour. . . . Next day, shortly after midnight, as he had been watching a basketball game, the

President calls to ask if I would be Ruth Bader Ginsburg's sponsor.[3]

On June 14, 1993, Bill Clinton nominated Ruth Bader Ginsburg to be an associate justice of the Supreme Court. Judge Ginsburg generously credited my *New Republic* article for helping bring her over the finish line. "You planted the idea," Ginsburg wrote to me on June 18. "I'll try hard to develop it." In fact, the piece was a serendipity, a consequence of my being at the right place at the right time, and joining a chorus of unsolicited testimonials to Ginsburg supplied by many friends and admirers who were fortunate enough to have gotten to know her.

For the next twenty-five years, my correspondence with Justice Ginsburg was warm but intermittent. She would sometimes write when she agreed or disagreed with an article I had written, or to issue an invitation to an especially interesting opera. (At this point, we had a running joke that any performance by the Washington Opera that she loved "may not measure up to your high standards.")

On September 24, 1993, for example, a week and a half before her first sitting on the Supreme Court, she sent an invitation to a Washington Opera performance of *Anna Bolena,* adding:

> If I knew his work better, I would go as far as Samuel Barber with you. Chambers are in pretty good shape now, but wait a few weeks more. By the end of November, the new carpet should be down, the rooms repainted, and the works on loan from local museums, in place.
>
> For your lighter reading, I enclose a page from a less well-known magazine, *The Brearley School Summer Bulletin* 1993.

The publication had reproduced a page from her daughter, Jane's, high school yearbook from many years earlier, declaring Jane's "ambition: to see her mother appointed to the Supreme Court" and "will probably end up: appointing her mother to the Supreme Court."

The following year, Justice Harry Blackmun resigned from the Court, and President Clinton nominated Stephen Breyer to replace him. On July 22, Ginsburg wrote to me "as a home subscriber of late (at least the spouse of one)" with thoughts about two of my recent *New Republic* pieces: one about Breyer and one about a new biogra-

18

phy of Learned Hand, written by her law school mentor Gerald Gunther. "Gerry was my teacher at Columbia and has been a friend ever since. Steve will be both good and true," she wrote, continuing:

Hand used words so well, I am not distracted by his less impressive qualities, including his unwillingness to consider me (or any other female) for a clerkship. During my 1959 to 1961 S.D.N.Y. days, when I finished work early enough, I occupied the back seat on evenings my judge, Judge Palmieri, drove the great man home. I loved Hand's recitation and songs, especially his Gilbert and Sullivan repertoire. Gerry's book is all I hoped it would be, yes, altogether wonderful.

My Opera news. We attended a performance of *Don Giovanni* at Glyndebourne July 17. The place is lovely, the orchestra and singers, most excellent. Only the production (sick modern) fell short.

Later in her letter, she noted two recently decided Supreme Court cases that had particular resonance for her. The first was *Ibanez v. Florida Department of Business and Professional Regulation,* where Ginsburg, writing in part for a unanimous Court, held that the state of Florida had violated the First Amendment rights of Silvia Safille Ibanez, a lawyer and certified public accountant who truthfully advertised herself as a CPA despite the fact that she was working at a firm unlicensed by a Dickensian bureaucracy known as the Florida Board of Accountancy. Ginsburg was especially taken by Ibanez herself, who successfully argued her own Supreme Court case, taking time off from her job as an accounting instructor at the University of Central Florida. Ginsburg may also have been drawn to the fact that Ibanez was an accomplished singer who had once sung at the Vatican and in the Camerata chorus.[4] Her attention to these details about the woman's life, I would soon learn, was characteristic of Ginsburg's approach to cases, focusing always on the real-world challenges faced by individual men and women trying to define their life paths.

The second recent case, *Ratzlaf v. United States,* showed Ginsburg's civil libertarian sensibilities as well as her attention to how the law actually operates in real people's lives. Waldemar Ratzlaf, who had run up $160,000 in gambling debts, was charged with violating federal reporting laws when he tried to pay off $100,000 in cash. He claimed that he didn't know that the law required him to report to the Treasury all transactions over $10,000 and that he should not be held liable for his failure to report. Writing for a five-to-four majority, Ginsburg agreed, holding that to establish that Ratzlaf "willingly violated" the reporting laws, the government had to prove that he knew his conduct was unlawful, along with the specific intent to break the law. Writing for the four dissenters, Justice Blackmun held that ignorance of the law is no defense. Judge Pierre Leval, a senior judge on the U.S. Court of Appeals for the Second Circuit, had recently written to Ginsburg to praise the decision, saying that he had always instructed juries that the word *willfully* means "with a bad purpose to disobey or disregard the law." The previous year, he noted, he had a case involving two sisters, Colombian nationals who worked as house cleaners and lived in poverty. For several months, they had made deposits for their brother-in-law totaling $120,000. The sisters testified that they had no idea that their conduct was illegal. Leval agreed that they had no illegal purpose, and the two women were acquitted. Like Ginsburg, Leval focused on the practical effects of a constitutional ruling on the lives of actual people struggling to make ends meet.

In 1997, the *New York Times Magazine* asked me to write a profile of Justice Ginsburg as "The New Face of Liberalism" on the Supreme Court. When I wrote to ask her for an interview, she coyly demurred. "Like Scarlett," she wrote, "I'll think about it tomorrow." She then sent a handwritten note: "Dear Jeff, Re *NYT* — please don't. See items in folder Packet. Just say no now and I'll give you an exclusive interview in 2010. Thanks, RBG." The articles in the accompanying blue folder included letters to the journalist Joan Biskupic and the law professor Hunter Clark refusing requests for extended interviews on the grounds that, as Ginsburg put it to Clark in 1995, "I think it too soon . . . to take me up as a fit subject for a biography. I am about to begin only the third year in this wonderful job, and anticipate that much of the work of any significance from my pen is yet to come . . . The year 2003 might be right to consider embarking on an account of my life. There is also the problem of overload . . . I must be careful to conserve all the hours I need for the Court's heavy work, also for the sleep essential to keep me going."

I persisted with the *New York Times* article nevertheless, and Ginsburg offered a unique solution to the challenge of granting me the access necessary to create an opening scene for the piece without granting me an interview. She invited me to her chambers and allowed me to look around, for as long as I liked. On the appointed day, after greeting me briefly, Ginsburg simply disappeared. Here is my account of the unusual experience that resulted.

Finding myself alone, I perused her bookshelves with some embarrassment. There were many books about civil procedure; but there were also a surprising number of popular books about contemporary feminism, including Deborah Tannen's *Talking from 9 to 5* and Anita Hill and Emma Jordan's *Race, Gender and Power in America.* There was a shrine to Puccini, with Art Nouveau posters from the early 20th century. Soon Justice Ginsburg's secretary walked in. The Justice had telephoned from the car, she said, and wanted to call my attention to one photograph in particular. It shows her son-in-law with her infant grandson. That, the Justice wanted me to know, was her dream for the future.

At the time, I took the comment to be a platitude about the joys of grandchildren; but later I realized that Justice Ginsburg may have been saying something more subtle about the transformation of sex roles. Soon after she joined the Court, I recalled, she had introduced herself, as new Justices traditionally do, by granting an interview to *The Docket Sheet,* a newsletter for Court employees. Toni House, the Court's public-information officer, asked her why she had agreed to a flexible schedule for one of her law clerks, David Post. Ginsburg replied that when Post applied for a clerkship, he was caring for his two small children during the day, so that his wife could sustain a demanding job as an economist. "I thought, 'This is my dream of the way the world should be,' " Ginsburg enthused. "When fathers take equal responsibility for the care of their children, that's when women will be truly liberated."[5]

The *New York Times Magazine* profile was notable for two lapses. It began by describing a recent conversation with Justice Ginsburg at the Washington Opera during the intermission of a production of Mozart's *Così fan tutte.* The opera is about two men who make a bet that their girlfriends will be faithful. They disguise themselves and discover that the women aren't faithful after all. Trying to add a feminist twist, the director had suggested that the women overhear the bet and simply pretend to be unfaithful. I suggested to Justice Ginsburg that this wasn't consistent with the sexual double standards of the eighteenth century, reflected in one traditional translation of the title: "Never Trust a Woman." Ginsburg responded that the Italian title was in the third-person plural. "They Are All Like That" would be a more accurate translation, she suggested. Therefore, there was no reason to suppose that Mozart and his librettist, Lorenzo Da Ponte, thought women any more or less trustworthy than men.

Although an admirable attempt to unite Ginsburg's love of Mozart with her commitment to gender equality, the anecdote turned out to be not quite right. After the article was published, Ginsburg sent me one of the copious letters she had received from music lovers across the country noting that *tutte* in Italian is feminine, as opposed to the masculine *tutti*. As a Harvard musicologist wrote to Ginsburg, "unlike English, Italian has gendered endings in the third person plural . . . so an even more accurate translation would be: 'Women all behave that way.' " With good humor, she called the letter the "best of my Italian collection."

The responsibility for the second lapse in the *Times* piece was entirely mine. The nationalist conservative commentator Pat Buchanan had attacked Ginsburg as a judicial activist during the 1996 presidential campaign, and on March 4 of that year, Ginsburg sent me the same response she had sent to a law professor and former colleague: "Appreciating how 'conservative' I am, you must be amused by Pat Buchanan's placement of me high on his 'hit' list. I know I owe it all to the last name Ginsburg. Still, I am honored to be in such good company."

In the article, I argued that Buchanan had it backward: judged by the small number of federal laws she had voted to strike down, Ginsburg was the most restrained judge on the Court. My lack of imagination in the piece was in predicting that Ginsburg would continue to define herself as a minimalist justice, a judicial priest rather than a judicial prophet: "The same qualities that make it very unlikely that Ginsburg will ever be a visionary leader as an Associate Justice — her minimalism, her jurisprudential as well as personal restraint and her emphasis on avoiding constitutional conflicts rather than engaging them — might make her an effective Chief Justice for a divided Court."

My prediction proved to be shortsighted. It wasn't Clinton who had the chance to appoint the next chief justice, but George W. Bush, as a result of *Bush v. Gore,* a decision that Ginsburg deplored. After Chief Justice William H. Rehnquist and Justice Sandra Day O'Connor were replaced by Chief Justice John G. Roberts Jr. and Justice Samuel A. Alito Jr., the Court moved to the right; and when Justice John Paul Stevens retired in 2010, Ginsburg became the senior liberal associate justice. In this new role, she would transform herself into the "Notorious RBG." And like her friend Justice Scalia, she became the visionary leader of the opposition.

When Justice Ginsburg was nominated to the Supreme Court in 1993, she was viewed as a judge's judge, a judicial minimalist, praised by conservatives (and questioned by some liberals) for her restrained approach to the judicial function. Over the next twenty-six years she has become one of the most inspiring American icons of our time and is now recognized as one of the most influential figures for constitutional change in American history. I had the chance to observe the transformation, and to ask her about it, in a series of public interviews and conversations we shared in my role as a legal journalist, a law professor, and, most recently, head of the National Constitution Center, in Philadelphia. Many of these interviews took place before audiences. In the conversations that follow, Ginsburg is always entirely herself — candid, composed, focused, listening intently, and astonishing in her recall of facts, legal arguments, cases, and the details of the human stories behind them. Above all, she is always deeply wise and thinks carefully before she speaks. (All her friends and law clerks have learned to sit serenely during the long pauses between a question and an answer because it's in the pauses that she is collecting her thoughts.) She demurs at the suggestion that she has changed during her time as a justice, insisting instead that the Court has become more conservative and that her role on the Court changed, too, after she became the senior liberal associate justice, responsible for assigning some majority opinions and many dissents. Nevertheless, she progressed from what she called the "flaming feminist" and brilliant strategist of the 1970s, as she transformed our constitutional understanding of gender equality, to the restrained judicial minimalist of the 1980s and '90s, determined to allow social change generally to be driven by legislatures and by evolution in public opinion rather than by courts. Most recently, in the past decade, she has combined the strategic vision and crusading passion for liberty and equality of her advocacy days with a principled determination to defend the Court's limited but crucial role in checking the choices of the people's representatives when they clash with the Constitution.

The transcripts of the conversations that follow have been condensed and rearranged so that they are organized by theme, and edited by Justice Ginsburg for clarity and precision. But every one of the justice's inspiring words is entirely her own.

1
HER LANDMARK CASES

As co-founder of the American Civil Liberties Union's Women's Rights Project, Ruth Bader Ginsburg sought from 1972 to 1980 to persuade the Supreme Court that legislation apparently designed to benefit or protect women could often have the opposite effect. For this reason, she chose to represent a series of *male* plaintiffs who had been denied legal benefits designated for women. This visionary strategy forced the Court to articulate a standard of scrutiny for gender discrimination that could be applied neutrally to either sex. Her model was Thurgood Marshall, the pathbreaking advocate who successfully argued *Brown v. Board of Education,* the 1954 Supreme Court case that struck down school segregation. As the founder and first director-counsel of the NAACP Legal Defense Fund, Marshall pursued an incremental strategy, at first representing African Americans who had been denied access to segregated law schools before taking on segregation in other public educational institutions that affected more people. Ginsburg, inspired by Marshall's example, also decided to move incrementally. She represented plaintiffs with whom the male judges of the 1970s were most likely to identify.

Ginsburg often discussed with me the cases from what she called the "bad old days," when the Court repeatedly upheld distinctions on the basis of sex. These were the cases she set out to overturn. In one of them, *Hoyt v. Florida* (1961), Gwendolyn Hoyt was convicted of murder by an all-male jury. In an unsuccessful challenge to the gender-based exclusion of women from the jury pool, Hoyt was represented by one of Ginsburg's heroes, the feminist lawyer Dorothy Kenyon. Later, when Ginsburg briefed her first Supreme Court case, *Reed v. Reed,* she put the names of Kenyon and another pioneering lawyer and civil rights activist, Pauli Murray, on the brief.

Reed v. Reed involved a divorced couple, Sally and Cecil Reed, who had shared custody of their adopted son, Richard, known as Skip. One weekend, when Skip asked his mother if he could come home early from his father's house, Sally told him that the law required the boy to stay, and in despair he fatally shot himself.[1] Overcome with grief, Sally applied to be the administrator of her son's estate, but an Idaho court rejected her request, citing a state law providing that "of several persons claiming and equally entitled to administer, males must be preferred to females." In her appeal of Sally Reed's case, Ginsburg was principal author of a brief comparing sex discrimination to race discrimination and arguing that the Idaho law should be subject to the same "strict scrutiny" standard as race discrimination, because sex and race were both "congenital, unalterable" traits "with no necessary relationship to talent or ability to perform." Ginsburg also argued that because Cecil and Sally Reed were "similarly situated," either could administer the estate equally well. On November 22, 1971, a unanimous Supreme Court, in an opinion by Chief Justice Warren Burger, struck down the Idaho law, for the first time invoking the Equal Protection Clause of the Fourteenth Amendment to the Constitution to invalidate discrimination on the basis of sex. But the victory was not complete. The Court had invalidated the statute because it imposed an "arbitrary legislative choice," choosing not to apply the "strict scrutiny" standard of gender-based discrimination that Ginsburg thought the Constitution required.

In another case, *Frontiero v. Richardson,* Ginsburg argued that the husbands of servicewomen deserved the same benefits as the wives of servicemen. When Sharon Frontiero, a physical therapist at an air force hospital in Montgomery, Alabama, got married, she was surprised to find that, unlike her male colleagues in the air force, who could claim their wives as "dependents" regardless of whether they actually depended on their husbands for support, she had not received the increased housing allowance that the men received when they married. Under the law, servicewomen could receive the increased housing allowance only if they proved they were contributing more than half the living expenses of their husbands.

Ginsburg argued that instead of cutting off the benefit for men who got married, the allowance should be extended to both sexes, following Justice Harlan's reasoning in *Welsh v. United States* that extension is just as valid a remedy as invalidation. She also made clear that the current policy penalized male spouses of female service members. Her oral argument was so powerful that the justices did not once interrupt her with questions, and in May 1973 the Court struck down the gender distinction, with a plurality of the justices indicating that they were willing to subject sex-based classifications to strict judicial scrutiny. The fifth vote for "strict scrutiny" never materialized, however, and in *Craig v. Boren* (1976), Ginsburg persuaded the Court to compromise on a standard known as "intermediate scrutiny" and to treat gender-based discrimination only slightly less skeptically than race-based discrimination.

One of Ginsburg's favorite cases as an advocate was *Weinberger v. Wiesenfeld* (1975), in which she represented a young widower who had been denied the Social Security survivor's benefits for which he would have qualified if he had been female, and which would have enabled him to remain at home to care for his infant son. The law appeared to discriminate against men alone, but Ginsburg argued successfully that the discrimination was, in fact, "double-edged": it relied on "archaic stereotypes" of men as breadwinners and women as caregivers; while the law required women to pay the same Social Security taxes as men, it gave fewer benefits to their families. The Supreme Court unanimously agreed.

Ginsburg and I spoke frequently over the years about the human stories behind her landmark cases during her time at the ACLU. She viewed her advocacy not as a crusade for abstract principles but as a fight for justice for individual men and women disadvantaged by laws that discriminated on the basis of sex. In describing the cases, she always combined remarkable precision about the technicalities of the law and the details of the facts with concern for the human beings involved.

JR: When you were an ACLU litigator in the seventies, you were called the Thurgood Marshall of the women's movement.

RBG: He was my model as a lawyer. You mentioned that I took a step-by-step, incremental approach. Well, that's what he did. He didn't come to the Court on day one and say, "End apartheid in America." He started with law schools and universities, and until he had those building blocks, he didn't ask the Court to end separate but equal. Of course, there was a huge difference between the litigation for gender equality in the seventies and the civil rights struggles in the fifties and sixties. The difference between Thurgood Marshall and me, most notably, is that my life was never in danger. His was. He would go to a southern town to defend people, some of them falsely accused, and he literally didn't know whether he would be alive at the end of the day. I never faced that kind of problem.

JR: How much did your experience with the ACLU influence the kind of justice you became?

RBG: When I was writing briefs for the ACLU Women's Rights Project, I tried to write them so that a justice who agreed with me could write his opinion from the brief. I conceived of myself in large part as a teacher. There wasn't a great understanding of gender discrimination. People knew that race discrimination was an odious thing, but there were many who thought that all the gender-based differentials in the law operated benignly in women's favor. So, my objective was to take the Court step by step to the realization, in Justice Brennan's words, that the pedestal on which some thought women were standing all too often turned out to be a cage.

JR: And you're taking a similar approach in

your dissenting opinions today?

RBG: My dissenting opinions, like my briefs, are intended to persuade. And sometimes one must be forceful about saying how wrong the Court's decision is.

JR: Let's talk about the laws you were able to chip away at during your time at the ACLU. Can you walk me through some of the most important victories?

RBG: Every one of these cases involved a law based on the premise that men earned the family's bread and women tended to the home and children. *Wiesenfeld* is probably the best illustration. The plaintiff, Stephen Wiesenfeld, was a man whose wife died in childbirth. He wanted to care personally for his infant, so he sought the child-in-care Social Security benefits that would enable him to do so. But those benefits were available only for widows, not widowers. Wiesenfeld's wage-earning wife had paid the same Social Security taxes that a man paid. But they netted less protection for her family. The male spouse was disadvantaged as a parent. We were trying to get rid of all laws modeled on that stereotypical view of the world, that men earn the bread and women take care of the home and children.

Stephen Wiesenfeld's wife was a teacher. She had a very healthy pregnancy. She was in the classroom until the ninth month. She went to the hospital to give birth, and the doctor tells Stephen, "You have a healthy baby boy, but your wife died of an embolism." And Stephen Wiesenfeld vowed that he would work only part-time until his son was in school full-time. So he applied for the Social Security benefits that he thought were available when a wage earner dies and leaves a child in the care of the surviving parent. He went to his Social Security office and was told, "Sorry, Mr. Wiesenfeld, that benefit is a mother's benefit, and you are not a mother." The point was: the woman paid her Social Security taxes; the government did not extend to her family the same protection it would extend to a man's family. The man doesn't have the choice to be a caregiving parent. He doesn't get any help when his life partner has died. We were attacking the notion that men don't take care of children, and women are not real wage earners; they are, at most, pin money earners.

JR: How did the Court rule?

RBG: The Court's judgment was unanimous, although the justices divided three ways on the reasons. Some said it's obviously discrimination against the woman as wage earner. She pays the same Social Security taxes as men pay, but the law doesn't give her family the same protection. Some thought it was discrimination against the man as parent. And one, Justice Rehnquist, said this is totally arbitrary from the point of view of the baby. Why should the baby have the opportunity for the care of a sole surviving parent when the parent is female, but not when the parent is male? We were confronting the justices with real-life situations so they could understand that what they once thought was a system operating benignly in women's favor in fact disadvantaged them. Even in Stephen Wiesenfeld's case — why was the law that way? Because women were thought to be the caregivers, the caregivers of the child. The aim was to break down the stereotypical view of men's roles and women's roles.

JR: You're not a fan of paternalistic stereotypes.

RBG: No.

JR: And when you litigated those cases, you faced male judges who had many of those stereotypical views, and you decided, therefore, to represent male plaintiffs, because you thought that they could better empathize with guys like them.

RBG: Well, I had at least as many — more women plaintiffs than men plaintiffs. We were trying to educate the Court that pigeonholing people because they are a woman or because they are a man, to say, "Men can be a doctor, lawyer, Indian chief, but girls can keep the house clean and take care of the children" — there's something wrong with that view of the world, a man's world with small space in it for woman, relegated to her own confined corner. Our argument: don't stereotype people because they are male or because they are female. Recognizing that the stereotype might well be true for the vast majority of people, but there are people who don't fit the mold, and they should be allowed to make choices, to live their lives without being pigeonholed because of their sex.

JR: What was the world like when you started litigating your cases in the 1960s?

RBG: Young people today have no idea what the world was like then. Women were either not called at all for jury duty, or given an automatic excuse. Under the law, "any woman" could be excused from jury duty. Dorothy Kenyon's mission was to end the differential treatment of men and women for jury service purposes, and she had the perfect case, *Hoyt v. Florida.*

Gwendolyn Hoyt, a woman from Hillsborough County, Florida, had a bitter dispute with her philandering, abusive husband and was humiliated to the breaking point. She spied her young son's baseball bat in the corner of the room, seized it, and with all her might hit her husband over the head. He fell against the hard floor. End of the altercation, beginning of the murder prosecution.

She was tried in Hillsborough County, Florida, where they didn't put women on the jury roll. Women could come to the clerk's office and volunteer. Hoyt's idea was: if I have women on this jury, maybe they're not going to acquit me, but maybe they will better understand my state of mind and convict me of the lesser crime of manslaughter instead of murder. Well, she was convicted of murder by an all-male jury, and her case came to the Supreme Court in

1961. We are now in the years of the "liberal Warren Court." They didn't get it.

JR: What happened to Gwendolyn Hoyt at the Supreme Court?

RBG: The argument in the Supreme Court was that she didn't have the opportunity for a jury drawn from a cross section of the population because half the population was left out. The Supreme Court said that law was simply reflecting women's place at the center of home and family life.

The Court's response was: "We don't understand this complaint. Women have the best of all possible worlds. They can serve if they want to, they don't have to serve if they don't want to." You can imagine Gwendolyn Hoyt: "What about me, you know, and my right to have a jury of my peers?" That case, lost in 1961, was an easy win in the seventies, before the not-so-liberal Burger Court. Why? Because society had changed. Because women had woken up. Because there was a worldwide movement, the UN had declared 1975 International Women's Year. It was that societal change that the Court's decisions reflected in the gender discrimination cases of the seventies.

JR: Tell me more about the state of gender discrimination law in the 1960s.

RBG: Rights were alive across the land in the sixties as a result of the civil rights movement, but the United States Supreme Court had never, in its entire history, held any classification based on gender unconstitutional.

One of my favorite cases from the not-so-good old days is *Goesaert v. Cleary,* a 1948 decision. A woman owned a tavern, and her daughter was her bartender. The state of Michigan passed a law that said women could not tend bar unless they were married to, or the daughter of, a male tavern owner. Well, that meant that these two women would be put out of business. The Supreme Court made light of that case, starting out with talking about Chaucer's old alewife. Instead of saying yes, women are perfectly capable of tending bar, the Court said women need to be protected. Bars are sometimes unpleasant; bad things can go on there.

To their great credit, the Michigan alcoholic beverages authority, after the Supreme Court said the law was okay, decided they were not going to enforce the law. So the Goesaerts were able to keep their tavern. In fact, when I went to law school, that case, *Goesaert v. Cleary,* was described in an abbreviated paragraph as one example of the Supreme Court letting go of its stranglehold on social and economic legislation. The ban on women bartending was described as health and safety legislation, a measure to protect women from the rowdy drunks. The Supreme Court justices never paused to recognize that the ban didn't apply to barmaids, the women who took drinks to the table and were much more in danger of the rowdy drunks than the woman standing behind the bar. That's where we were not so long ago.

JR: What was your first Supreme Court case?

RBG: Sally Reed's case was the first one. The law she attacked involved appointments as administrator of a decedent's estate. The law read, "As between persons equally entitled to administer a decedent's estate, males must be preferred to females." Sally Reed had a teenage son. She and her husband were divorced. When the child was young — the legal term is "of tender years" — Sally was given custody. Then the boy becomes a teenager, and the father said,

"Now he needs to be prepared for a man's world, so I would like to be the custodian." The family court said yes, and Sally was disconsolate; she thought the father would be a very bad influence on the boy. Sadly, she was right. The boy was sorely depressed. He took out one of his father's many rifles and committed suicide.

Sally wanted to be appointed administrator of his estate. There was no economic advantage to her in this; it was for sentimental reasons. And then the father applied two weeks later, and the probate judge said, "I'm sorry, Sally, I have no choice. The law says men must be preferred to women." Well, Sally Reed thought she had experienced an injustice. She was an everyday person who made her living by taking care of elderly and infirm people in her home. She thought an injustice had been done and that the laws of the United States would protect her from the injustice. She went through three levels of the Idaho court system, on her own dime. She had retained a lawyer from Boise, Idaho, Allen Derr, to represent her. Hers was the turning-point case in the Supreme Court — nothing that the National Organization for Women or the ACLU had generated as a test case. Sally Reed was among the women across the country waking up to the inequality to which they had been exposed, for which there was no rhyme or reason.

When Sally Reed's case came to the Court, she won unanimously. For the first time in its history, the Supreme Court in 1971 held a law unconstitutional because it discriminated arbitrarily against women. One of the notable things about that case, as I just said, Sally Reed was an everyday woman. She financed the case on her own dime, all through three levels of the Idaho courts. She believed we had a justice system that would vindicate her right to be treated equally. There were people all over the country, in the civil rights movement of the sixties, in the revived feminist movement in the seventies, who trusted our system's ability to right an injustice.

JR: So that suggests the courts cannot do it alone. It really has to be society that comes to accept this new vision of equality before it can change.

RBG: Absolutely, Jeff. One of the features of the Reed brief — it was argued and decided at the end of 1971 — we put on the cover, as counsel, two women's names, Pauli Murray and Dorothy Kenyon. They were women of the generation before mine who in the forties and fifties were saying exactly the same things we were saying in the seventies, but society wasn't ready to listen.

JR: Tell me about the *Frontiero* case.

RBG: She told it best herself: Lieutenant Sharron Frontiero got married, went to the personnel office at the air force base where she was stationed, and asked for the married officer's housing allowance and access to medical facilities on base for her husband. She couldn't believe what she was told: *Those benefits are not available to me. Why? Because I'm a woman, they're available only to men.* Sharron thought she lived in a system where that kind of thing shouldn't happen, and that courts could right the wrong she encountered. I will be on a panel with Sharron Frontiero, now Cohen, in Omaha in August 2020, as part of a celebration of the ratification of the Nineteenth Amendment.

JR: You've seen her again since the case?

RBG: Yes, and we correspond from time to time. We met some years ago in Asheville,

North Carolina, for a program on women's progress sponsored by women lawyers and jurists in North Carolina, South Carolina, and Georgia. Stephen Wiesenfeld was one of the participants, also the women who sued the navy for not assigning women to sea duty.

JR: I hear you talk about these cases, and they're not abstractions to you. You know the women and the men; you know their stories. It's not an intellectual feast or an academic exercise. You really are caring about the parties and noticing what's going on.

RBG: Yes, and one of the things about the gender discrimination cases in the seventies — none of these were test cases in the sense that some ideological organization said, "We want to bring this issue to the Court, and let's see if we can find a case." These were people like Stephen Wiesenfeld, like Sharron Frontiero, Sally Reed.

I'm regularly in touch with Stephen Wiesenfeld. I officiated at his son Jason's wedding many years ago. Jason went to Columbia Law School, changed to investment banking, is now the father of three children. Stephen at last found the second

love of his life, and I recently officiated at
the Court at his second marriage ceremony.

2
MARRIAGE BETWEEN EQUALS

Before I asked Justice Ginsburg to officiate at my marriage in the fall of 2017, I brought my fiancée, Lauren, to a meeting in her chambers at the Supreme Court so the justice could get to know her. She listened closely to Lauren's descriptions of her current work as a professor of cultural anthropology, studying law and the crisis of constitutional democracy in Ghana. Justice Ginsburg spoke, intently and expansively, about her admiration for the South African Constitution, which she had recommended as a better model than the U.S. Constitution for the drafters of the Egyptian Constitution after the Arab Spring in 2011. The South African document includes explicit protections for abortion rights, health care, and minimizing income inequality.

At the end of the conversation, she agreed to perform our marriage in her chambers. Before we returned for the ceremony a month later, she sent us drafts of the vows for wedding ceremonies she had performed for other friends, suggesting we might want to incorporate parts of them as we prepared our own script. The drafts began with the justice offering a description of marriage as a partnership between equals, as in her own fifty-six-year marriage to Marty Ginsburg.

Your commitment is rooted in a deep appreciation of each other's talents and experiences. You have learned the importance of patience, of good humor, and of the joy you bring each other. May the love you bear, each for the other, ever make of the two of you magically more — wiser and richer in experience, happier than either would be alone.

The sample vows ended with the traditional blessing: "Jeffrey, you may kiss the bride."

We incorporated these suggestions into our draft script, adding poems we had chosen to consecrate our marriage. We then sent the draft back to her for review.

Justice Ginsburg is a legendary copy editor and deadline enforcer, and she corrects typos and word choices on the drafts of her Supreme Court colleagues with rigor, precision, and speed. Several hours after receiving our draft, she sent it back with tracked changes. She had edited the last sentence in this way:

Jeffrey, ~~you may kiss the bride.~~ and Lauren, you may embrace each other for the first kiss of your marriage.

The change exemplified a combination of a close attention to detail with a determination to endorse an ever-expanding vision of gender equality in a changing world. She had delivered the more traditional blessing hundreds of times, but reading it anew, she decided to alter it to reflect a more egalitarian vision. And the care she took to change the script (within hours, at the beginning of a Supreme Court term) shows her iron self-discipline, her care for expressing herself in precisely the right words, and her warm interest in the personal details of the lives of her friends, family, colleagues, and the litigants she once represented.

All these qualities were evident in her storied marriage to Marty Ginsburg. The two met at Cornell University in the fall of 1950. Marty saw Ruth on campus and convinced his roommate, who was dating her friend, to arrange a blind date. They soon bonded over their love of classical music and their respect for each other's intelligence. "He was the only guy I ever dated who cared whether I had a brain," Ruth would later declare. "He was just so damn smart."[1] Marty was called into service in the army early in their marriage, after his first year of law school, and spent two years teaching artillery at Fort Sill, Oklahoma. Their daughter, Jane, was born there in 1955, fourteen months before Marty and Ruth set out together for Harvard Law School, where the dean, Erwin Griswold, asked Ruth at an opening reception, "Why are you at Harvard Law School, taking a place that could have gone to a man?" Ruth replied that it was important for a wife to understand her husband's work.[2] After Marty graduated and got a job in New York, Ruth transferred to Columbia for her final year of law school, where she finished tied for first in her class. Their son, James, was born in 1965. Marty's career as a tax lawyer thrived, and Ruth became a law professor at Rutgers and later at Columbia, while also serving as the head of the ACLU's Women's Rights Project. When James's school repeatedly called her whenever he got into scrapes, she replied that the boy had two parents and that Marty should be called as well.

(After that suggestion, she reports, the calls came barely once a term.) The school was not worried about taking a woman away from her paid work, but was hesitant to interrupt a man at work.

From her days as an advocate to her days as a justice, Ginsburg insisted that men and women would be truly equal only when they took equal responsibility for child rearing. She wrote as early as 1972 that "child rearing, as distinguished from child bearing, does not involve a physical characteristic unique to one sex," noting that Sweden's Commission on Family Policy had recently proposed to replace existing laws that gave working women the right to six months of "childbirth" leave with an eight-month leave that either parent could take or both could divide.[3]

I had the great pleasure of spending time with the Ginsburgs over the years and was always struck by how much in love they remained. Marty made Ruth, and everyone else, laugh out loud with his whimsical humor, which was often based on a series of gags that he, in fact, was as famous as his wife. He told his grandchildren, for example, that the statue on the top of the U.S. Capitol was of him, and when Ruth received a standing ovation at the opera, he whispered that he hadn't realized there was a tax lawyers' convention in town to cheer him on.

In a 1995 speech, "Reflections on Supreme Court Spousehood," Marty joked, "As far as I can tell based on only twenty-four months' experience, the only duty of a Supreme Court spouse is to avoid stupidity in public appearances. This is not always an easy task." He then offered up an all-purpose form letter that he had drafted for his wife to send to all correspondents requesting her assistance.

To help the Justice stay above water, we have endeavored to explain why she cannot do what you have asked her to do. Please refer to the paragraph below with the caption that best fits your request.

Favorite Recipe. The Justice was expelled from the kitchen a quarter-century ago by her food-loving children. She no longer cooks, and the one recipe from her youth, Tuna Fish Casserole, is nobody's favorite.

Photograph. Justice Ginsburg is flattered, indeed amazed, by the number of requests for her photograph. She is now sixty-two years of age, and understandably keeps no supply.

Are We Related? The birth names of the Justice's parents are Bader and Amster. Many who bear those names have written, giving details of origin and immigration. While the information is engrossing, you and she probably are not related within any reasonable degree of consanguinity.

After going on in this vein, Marty concluded: "Ruth's secretaries, you will not be surprised to learn, vetoed my letter. Amazingly, since that time they have managed to cope."[4]

I last saw Marty at the Washington Opera, soon after his cancer reemerged in 2008; he was as witty as ever and produced a quip so funny that he made the justice and me laugh out loud. (I wish I could remember what it was.) In June 2010, after Marty learned that his cancer was inoperable, he wrote this soul-stirring love letter to Ruth:

My dearest Ruth–
You are the only person I have loved in my life, setting aside, a bit, parents and kids, and their kids. And I have admired and loved you almost since the day we first met at Cornell. . . .
What a treat it has been to watch you

57

progress to the very top of the legal world.

I will be in JH Medical Center until Friday, June 25, I believe, and between then and now, I shall think hard on my remaining health and life, and whether on balance the time has come for me to tough it out or to take leave of life because the loss of quality now simply overwhelms.

I hope you will support where I come out, but I understand you may not. I will not love you a jot less.

Marty[5]

He died at home the following Sunday, June 27.

Justice Ginsburg was back at work at the Supreme Court the next day, for the last week of the term. I interviewed her onstage at the Aspen Ideas Festival just a few weeks later. Her grandson, Paul, who accompanied her on the trip, was sitting in the front row.

JR: You're very strong to be here. You've just lost your beloved Marty, our dear friend, and I want to express condolences on behalf of everyone here. I met you both first about twenty years ago, and you know what an inspiration he was to me and everyone who knew him as a model of the perfect husband in a truly equal partnership. He had daunting skills. First of all, he could cook like a dream. He would make these incredible desserts and dinners. He shared in child rearing at a time when that was not fashionable. He was incredibly funny and made you laugh out loud whenever you were with him. And most important, both of you were so crazy about each other. You were so visibly in love that just being near you was always a joy. People want to know the secret to this remarkably happy marriage. Why don't you share some of your secrets?

RBG: Marty and I lived happily together for fifty-six years. And on the division of labor in our household, my daughter was asked by a reporter, soon after my nomination, "Well, tell me, what is life like in your house?" And she said, "Well, my father does the cooking, and my mother does the thinking." Not true at all, because Marty was the smartest man I knew. Marty attributes his skills in the kitchen to two women — one was his mother, and the second, his wife.

JR: It's a time of such anxiety, the political system is so polarized, men and women are figuring out how to interact with each other. What is your advice about how civil interactions are possible? And I do want you to share the advice that you've given to so many couples you have married. Explain what the lesson is, because it's profound and very wise.

RBG: Well, I had a remarkable mother-in-law, Marty's mother. I was married in my husband's home, and just before the ceremony, my mother-in-law took me aside and said, "I'd like to tell you the secret of a happy marriage."

"I'll be glad to know what it is."

She said, "Dear, in every good marriage, it helps sometimes to be a little deaf."

And that is advice I have applied not only in fifty-six years of marriage, but, to this day, in my current workplace. If an unkind word is said, you just tune out.

JR: It's a profound lesson about never reacting in anger, always maintaining your equanimity, and if others lose their temper, not losing yours.

RBG: Well, emotions like anger, remorse, and jealousy are not productive. They will not accomplish anything, so you must keep them under control. In the days when I was a flaming feminist litigator, I never said to judges who asked improper questions, "You sexist pig."

I'll tell you one such incident. I was arguing a case in Trenton, New Jersey, before a three-judge federal district court, and one judge remarked, "Well, women are doing fine these days. Opportunities are equal for them everywhere. Even in the military they have equal opportunity."

I responded, "Your honor, flight training isn't available to women."

His comeback: "Oh, don't tell me that. Women have been in the air forever. I know from experience with my own wife and daughter."

So how do I react? "I've met some men who don't have their feet planted firmly on the ground."

Comments like that judge's are rarely heard nowadays. But in the seventies, when judges knew it was improper to make racist jokes, women were still fair game.

JR: What drew you to Marty when you first met?

RBG: Sandra Day O'Connor has talked about the age when we were growing up.

Marty was most unusual. He was the first boy I ever met who cared that I had a brain. And he always thought I was better than I thought I really was.

I mean, this was a man — incidentally, he was in the army for two years, so he left law school after his first year. By the time, two years later, when we went back to school, Marty to the second year, me to the first year, Jane was born. I started law school when Jane was fourteen months. The dean of the law school then, Erwin Griswold — many of you know him; he was a great law school dean and then a great solicitor general — but when he would introduce me or in social conversation, he would say I had met Marty in law school, and that Marty was a year ahead of me, so I transferred to Columbia for my third year. I finally said one day, "Dean Griswold, it's embarrassing to me, because Jane was four years old when I graduated from law school." But the notion of Harvard Law School and motherhood mixing was beyond the pale. In my entering class at Harvard, there were nine women and over five hundred men. A big jump over Marty's class, which had five women and over five hundred men. The notion that you could go through that rigorous training in law school and care for an infant — the two just didn't mix in the dean's mind.

JR: Well, these questions are central to gender equality, and you have, or did a few years ago, a picture in your chambers along these lines. It's of your son-in-law holding your grandson.

RBG: It's my grandson, Paul, when he was two months old. He's on a bed with his father, who is looking at Paul with such tremendous love. And so that's my ideal: a child should have two caring parents, and if every child could grow up with a father and a mother, both of whom love and care for the child, ours would be a much better world.

JR: You once told me, referring to that picture, you said, "That's my hope for the future." And at first I thought it was sort of a platitude. I didn't know what you were saying. But I realized you were saying your hope for the future was that men assume equal responsibility with women for child rearing — then women will be truly equal.

RBG: Yes. My daughter took the photograph. The love of that father for that infant is communicated so beautifully in that photograph, which is kept in a prime place in my chambers.

JR: When it comes to men and women taking equal responsibility for child care, are we doing better now than we were ten or twenty years ago?

RBG: We are doing a lot better. When I was in my last year of law school, I was attending Columbia Law School, my daughter was between three and four. There was only one nursery school in that entire area. They would take a child from nine to twelve [in the morning] or two to five [in the afternoon]. By the time my daughter was a mother herself, and teaching at Columbia Law School, there were over two dozen full-day daycare facilities in that area. A few of my law clerks have taken parental leave, male law clerks. It's more common than it once was.

My very first year on the Court, I was served by a law clerk who had been with me on the DC Circuit, and his application was tremendously attractive to me. Why? Because he wrote that he was studying law at night at Georgetown, and the reason was that his wife, an economist, had a good job at the World Bank. That and one other thing. He submitted as his writing sample his first-year-of-law-school writing exercise, and it was the theory of contract as illustrated in Wagner's Ring Cycle.

I asked the chief justice — this is way back, in 1993 and 1994 — if the clerk could have access to [the legal research services] Westlaw and Lexis at home. And Chief Justice Rehnquist said no, the law clerks were expected to stay on the premises as long as necessary. The next year, all of the law clerks had access to Westlaw and Lexis at home.

JR: How optimistic are you about that vision of men and women sharing child responsibilities? Hanna Rosin wrote a cover story for the *Atlantic* called "The End of Men."[6] She points out that the attributes most valuable today — social intelligence, open communication, the ability to focus — are not predominantly male. She notes that in 2009, Iceland elected "the world's first openly lesbian head of state, who campaigned explicitly against the male elite she claimed had destroyed the nation's banking system and who vowed to 'end the age of testosterone.' " You managed to convince the Court to accept gender equality, step by step. Are you as optimistic as Hanna Rosin that women are outstripping men, and that men are going to step up to the plate and take responsibility for children?

RBG: I think that men and women, shoulder to shoulder, will work together to make this a better world. Just as I don't think that men are the superior sex, neither do I think women are. I think it's great that we're beginning to use the talent of all of the people in all walks of life, and that we no longer have the closed doors that we once had.

JR: Are you satisfied with women's achievements? I mean, there are conflicting statistics, in this article: on the one hand, women are 60 percent of all college graduates and hold 60 percent of all master's degrees; on the other hand, only 3 percent of Fortune 500 CEOs are women. Do we have further to go?

RBG: Of course we have further to go, but there has been huge progress. Progress comes slowly, and one must be patient. I remember the first time I heard about the Swedish parental leave system. They had it long before we did. Someone commenting on it said, "But only 10 percent of the fathers take that leave." And I said, "Well, 10 percent is better than 2 percent." It is frankly more than I thought it would be in the beginning. And that's, I think, how it is shaping up today. More and more men are sharing the joys as well as the burdens of bringing up the next generation, but it takes time. The best way I found to reach men of a certain age in the days when I was a flaming feminist was to have them think about their daughters, and what they would like the world to be like for their daughters.

JR: And norms are changing. Hanna Rosin reports that the "mommy track" is giving way to a demand for flex-time among both men and women who are graduating from college. That's a prized employment perk, to be able to have a flexible schedule, and both men and women want it.

RBG: And you would think it should be ever so much easier in the electronic age when you have, for example, the entire law library at your fingertips at home.

In September 2013, I interviewed Justice Ginsburg at the National Constitution Center, and she mentioned another marriage she had performed the previous week.

JR: You recently performed a historic marriage that took place in Washington. Tell us about that. That was the first same-sex marriage performed by a U.S. Supreme Court justice.

RBG: Yes, it was the marriage of Michael Kaiser, who is the head of the Kennedy Center, to his longtime partner, whose name happens to be John Roberts, the same name as our chief justice. It was a simply beautiful wedding. The high point of the ceremony for me was Harolyn Blackwell, who sang "Du bist die Ruh." It was exquisite. There was lots of family on both sides — many Robertses, many Kaisers. It was a wedding of two people deeply in love with each other and at last able to make their shared lives a lawful relationship.

JR: And how did you feel as a justice performing the ceremony? What did it say about America?

RBG: It's one more example of what I see as the genius of our Constitution. If I asked you the question: Who counted among "We the People" when our Constitution was new? Well, not very many people. Certainly, I wouldn't count. Certainly not people who were held in human bondage. And not even most men, because you had to be a property owner as well. So think of what our nation and our Constitution have become over, now, well more than two centuries. The idea of "We the People" has become more and more embracive. People who were once left out, people who were once slaves, women, Native Americans, did not count in the beginning. Inclusiveness has come about as a result of constitutional amendments — in the case of the Civil War, three post–Civil War amendments — and judicial interpretation. The idea was there from the beginning: equality. And yet you can read every page of your pocket Constitution and you will not find, in the original Constitution, the word *equal,* or *equality,* even though equality was a main theme of the Declaration of Independence. The word *equal* becomes a part of the Constitution in the Fourteenth Amendment. So I see as the genius of our Constitution and of our society — how much more embracive we have become than we were at the start.

ROE

When she was nominated to the Supreme Court, the most controversial part of Ruth Bader Ginsburg's constitutional record was her criticism of the legal reasoning in *Roe v. Wade.* It inspired opposition from some feminist groups who objected to her argument that *Roe* had been decided too broadly, preventing public opinion from catching up to the courts. Ginsburg argued that if the Supreme Court in 1973 had simply struck down the Texas law at issue in the case and had resisted the temptation to impose a national framework for abortion, the case might have inspired less of a backlash, allowing a growing number of state legislatures to recognize a right to reproductive choice on their own.

What her feminist critics in the 1990s failed to appreciate was that Ginsburg was laying the groundwork for a firmer constitutional foundation for reproductive choice, one rooted in women's equality rather than the right to privacy. Expanding the arguments she had made as an advocate in the 1970s, Ginsburg maintained that restrictions on abortion are best understood not as a private matter between women and their male doctors; instead, the restrictions violate women's constitutional right to equality by limiting their ability to define their own life choices, imposing burdens that are not imposed on men. If *Roe v. Wade* had been based on the Equal Protection Clause of the Constitution instead of on the Due Process Clause, Ginsburg insisted, it would have been more constitutionally convincing.

Ginsburg's criticisms proved to be prophetic. In June 1992, the Supreme Court in *Planned Parenthood v. Casey* surprised liberals and conservatives by upholding *Roe* in an opinion that tacitly recognized that restrictions on abortion do indeed implicate concerns about women's equality as well as the right to privacy.

A few months later, Ginsburg published her Madison Lecture at New York University Law School, "Speaking in a Judicial Voice," the same lecture that President Clinton mentioned to Senator Moynihan as the basis for his concern that "women are against her." In the lecture, Ginsburg praised Justices Anthony Kennedy, Sandra Day O'Connor, and David Souter for acknowledging, in their opinion in *Casey,* the intimate connection between a woman's "ability to control [her] reproductive life" and her "ability . . . to participate equally in the economic and social life of the Nation." Ginsburg noted that women's equality was a less prominent theme in *Roe,* which had "coupled with the rights of the pregnant woman the free exercise of her physician's medical judgment," and she suggested that *Roe* might have been less controversial if the decision had focused more precisely on women's equality.

In the lecture, Ginsburg also criticized the "breathtaking" *Roe* opinion for its lack of caution. The justices had fashioned a sweeping set of regulations for the entire country instead of striking down the Texas abortion ban at issue in the case, which allowed exceptions only for lifesaving medical procedures, and inviting a dialogue with the state legislatures. "Suppose the Court had stopped there, rightly declaring unconstitutional the most extreme brand of law in the nation, and had not gone on, as the Court did in *Roe,* to fashion a regime blanketing the subject, a set of rules that displaced virtually every state law then in force," Ginsburg asked. "A less encompassing *Roe,* one that merely struck down the extreme Texas law and went no further on that day . . . might have served to reduce rather than to fuel controversy."[1] Ginsburg contrasted *Roe,* which galvanized the pro-life movement and provoked a legislative backlash, with the gender cases she litigated in the 1970s, which began a dialogue with the state legislatures, inviting them to move slowly in a more liberal direction. "In most of the post-1970 gender-classification cases, unlike *Roe,* the Court . . . approved the direction of change through a temperate brand of decisionmaking, one that was not extravagant or divisive," she concluded. "*Roe,* on the other hand, halted a political process that was moving in a reform direction and thereby, I believe, prolonged divisiveness and deferred stable settlement of the issue."[2]

The roots of Ginsburg's criticisms of *Roe* can be found in her litigation from the 1970s. Ginsburg first articulated her view that "disadvantageous treatment" on the basis of pregnancy is tantamount to sex discrimination in a 1972 case, *Struck v. Secretary of Defense.* Ginsburg challenged a regulation requiring all female air force personnel to be discharged as soon as they became pregnant. The regulation, Ginsburg argued, amounted to unconstitutional sex discrimination because it treated pregnancy far more harshly than it treated other temporary disabilities affecting men and women. Because the case became moot, Ginsburg was unable to convince the Court to adopt her view, but she had planted a seed.

Despite her criticisms of the sweep of *Roe*, Ginsburg never publicly questioned the constitutional foundations of the right to privacy itself. In her *Struck* brief, she noted that "individual privacy with respect to procreation and intimate personal relations is a right firmly embedded in this nation's tradition and in the precedents of this Court." And although Ginsburg criticized *Roe* for its immoderation, her alternative grounding for abortion rights is potentially more sweeping. In a 1984 speech at the University of North Carolina she argued explicitly that government has an affirmative duty to fund abortions for poor women. A federal law called the Hyde Amendment, which the Supreme Court upheld in 1980, violated the equality of poor women, she suggested, because it said that the government would subsidize all medically necessary procedures except for abortion. "If the Court had acknowledged a woman's equality aspect" to reproductive choice, she concluded, "a majority perhaps might have seen the public assistance cases as instances in which, borrowing a phrase from Justice Stevens, the sovereign had violated its 'duty to govern impartially.' "[3]

Ginsburg's central premise is that anti-abortion laws, like employment discrimination against pregnant women, are based on "stereotypical assumptions" about women as caregivers. Today, pro-choice scholars, advocates, and citizens, including millions of young women, have embraced her emphasis on equality, rather than privacy, as the soundest constitutional foundation for the right to choose.

Moreover, Ginsburg's prediction that the Supreme Court would chip away at *Roe* proved to be well founded. As she put it in her Madison Lecture, "Doctrinal limbs too swiftly shaped, experience teaches, may prove unstable."[4] The first sign of the retreat came in the 2007 case *Gonzales v. Carhart*, where the Supreme Court, in a five-to-four opinion written by Justice Kennedy, upheld the 2003 federal ban on what were called "partial-birth abortions." Ginsburg wrote a blistering dissent, calling Kennedy's decision "alarming" and criticizing in particular his claim that it was "self-evident" that women who had abortions might come to regret their decisions. "This way of thinking reflects ancient notions about women's place in the family and under the Constitution — ideas that have long since been discredited," Ginsburg wrote. She never forgot Kennedy's vote; when I wrote in the *New Republic* in 2011 that Kennedy "votes with the liberals on laws restricting abortion and gay rights," she wrote to me objecting: "You may be accurate (so far) about gay rights, but what of *Gonzales v. Carhart,* and before that, *Stenberg v. Carhart,*" where Kennedy dissented from the Court's five-to-four decision to strike down partial-birth abortion bans in the states? Still, Ginsburg always looked for consensus in abortion cases where she could find it. She joined the 2014 *McCullen v. Coakley* opinion, where the Court unanimously struck down a Massachusetts law establishing thirty-five-foot buffer zones around abortion clinics on the grounds that limiting abortion protests in this manner violated the First Amendment rights of protesters.

In our conversations, I asked Justice Ginsburg repeatedly whether she thought *Roe* would be overturned. After Justice

O'Connor's retirement in 2006, she said many times that she feared that *Roe* would be narrowed and that the greatest effect would be felt by poor women who lived in areas where access to abortion was already limited. But in 2018, a month after Justice Kennedy's retirement, she told me she was "skeptically hopeful" that the Court would not overturn landmark precedents with abandon and that the core of *Roe*'s protection for reproductive choice early in pregnancy would be preserved.

JR: Will *Roe v. Wade* be overturned?

RBG: This Court had an opportunity to do that in the *Casey* case. There was a strong opinion speaking for Justice O'Connor, Justice Kennedy, and Justice Souter, saying *Roe v. Wade* has been the law of the land since 1973, we respect precedent, and *Roe v. Wade* should not be overruled. If the Court sticks to that position, there will be no overruling, and it won't matter whether there's a Democratic president or a Republican president.

JR: And if *Roe* were overturned, how bad would the consequences be?

RBG: It would be bad for nonaffluent women. If we imagine the worst-case scenario, with *Roe v. Wade* overruled, there would remain many states that would not go back to the way it once was. It doesn't matter what Congress or the state legislatures do, there will be other states that provide this facility, and women will have access to it if they can pay for it. Women who can't pay are the *only* women who would be affected.

Roe v. Wade was decided in 1973. Two generations of young women have grown up understanding that they can control their own reproductive capacity and in fact their life's destiny. We will never go back to the way it once was. *Roe v. Wade,* in its time, was not all that controversial. It was a seven-to-two decision, only two dissenters. Even at the time of *Roe v. Wade,* there were four states where a woman who wanted an abortion, at least in the first trimester, could have access to a safe, legal abortion. And now, it would be a lot more than four states. What that means is any woman who has the wherewithal to travel, to take a plane, to take a train to a state that provides access to abortion, that woman will never have a problem. Any woman who has the means to travel from one state to another — you don't have to go to Japan or Cuba — will have access to a safe abortion. So it's the poor people — whatever the state legislation may be, whatever the Court may do — it is only poor women who will suffer, and I think that if people realize that, maybe they will have a different attitude.

JR: How can advocates make sure that poor women's access to reproductive choice is protected? Can legislatures be trusted, or is it necessary for courts to remain vigilant?

RBG: How could you trust legislatures in view of the restrictions states are imposing? Think of the Texas legislation that would put most clinics out of business. The courts can't be trusted, either. Think of the [*Gonzales v.*] *Carhart* decision going way back, to the two decisions that denied Medicaid coverage for abortion. I don't see this as a question of courts versus legislatures. In my view, both have been moving in the wrong direction. It will take people who care about poor women. The irony and tragedy is any woman of means can have a safe abortion somewhere in the United States. But women lacking the wherewithal to travel or to miss workdays can't. There is no big constituency out there concerned about access restrictions on poor women.

JR: How can that constituency be created?

RBG: For one thing, the advocacy of human rights groups can make a big difference. Going back to the 1980s, I was speaking at Duke, not about abortion in particular, but about equal opportunities for women to be whatever their God-given talent allowed them to be, without artificial barriers placed in their way. During the question period, an African American man commented: "We know what you lily-white women are all about. You want to kill black babies." That's how some in the African American community regarded the choice movement. So I think it would be helpful if civil rights groups homed in on the impact of the absence of choice on African American women. That would be useful.

Ultimately, the people have to organize themselves. Think of the Pregnancy Discrimination Act. The Court had said that discrimination on the basis of pregnancy was not discrimination on the basis of sex. A coalition was organized to get [the Pregnancy Discrimination Act] passed. The ACLU was the central player, but everyone was on board. It must start with the people.

Legislatures are not going to move without that kind of propulsion.

JR: This is a different version of the same question: What was the Court's error in *Roe,* and how can it avoid that sort of error in other cases?

RBG: The Texas law was the most extreme in the nation. A woman did not have access to an abortion unless it was necessary to save her life. It didn't matter that it would ruin her health, it didn't matter that the pregnancy was the result of a brutal rape or incest. So that case came to the Supreme Court, and the Supreme Court could simply have said, that's too extreme. That gives no credit at all to the woman's liberty, so it's unconstitutional, period. The great constitutional law scholar Paul Freund, when he was asked what he thought of the *Roe v. Wade* decision, said it's like the grandmother who trots out her grandson to impress her company and asks him, "Do you know how to spell banana?" And the child answers, "Yes, I know how to start, but I just don't know where to stop."

At the time of *Roe v. Wade,* this issue was all over the state legislatures. Sometimes, the choice people won, sometimes they lost, but they were out there organizing and getting political experience. The Supreme Court's decision made every law in the country, even the most liberal, unconstitutional in one fell swoop. So the people who prevailed said, "How great, we're done, we've got it all. The Supreme Court gave it to us." What happened? Opposition mounted, and instead of fighting in the trenches, state by state, to retain restrictive abortion laws, there was one clear target to aim at: the unelected justices of the Supreme Court. This is a decision that should be made, so the argument went, by the people's elected representatives and not nine, at the time, old men.

The law was in a state of flux. And there were many states, including my home state of New York, that allowed a woman to obtain a safe abortion in the first trimester, no questions asked. There were four states that were in that position; there were other states that had grounds permitting access to abortion — the woman's health, rape, incest. So the law was in a state of change. I think it would have been healthier for that change to have gone on. The Supreme Court would have struck down the most extreme law, then the states would react to that. The Court usually doesn't take giant steps. It moves incrementally. *Roe v. Wade* was a dramatic exception to that cautious way of operating.

JR: You criticized the Court in *Roe* for jumping ahead of public opinion.

RBG: The Court is a reactive institution. You react to the controversies that are brought to the Court. *Roe v. Wade,* I should be very clear — I think the result was absolutely right. Texas had the most extreme law in the nation; the Court could have decided the case before it, which is how the Court usually operates. It should have said that the Texas law is unconstitutional. There was no need to declare every law in the country addressing abortion, even the most liberal, unconstitutional. That's not the way the Court usually operates. It doesn't take giant steps.

Now I know many people think my judgment about that is wrong. I know there was a very strong Right to Life movement long before *Roe* came down; it continued after. But now there is a target that was not there before *Roe v. Wade.*

Another aspect of my criticism: the image you get from reading the *Roe v. Wade* opinion is it's mostly a doctor's rights case

— a doctor's right to prescribe what he thinks his patient needs. And the images of the doctor and the little woman — it's never the woman alone. It's always the woman in consultation with her doctor. My idea of how choice should have developed was not a privacy notion, not a doctor's right notion, but a woman's right to control her own destiny, to be able to make choices without a Big Brother state telling her what she can and cannot do.

JR: That has been your great contribution to the jurisprudence of gender equality. Will the Court, do you think eventually, someday, recognize abortion rights as a question involving gender discrimination?

RBG: Well, I think that theme is already sounded in the *Casey* decision. The Court had an opportunity to overturn *Roe v. Wade,* but it said, "No, generations have grown up understanding — girls have grown up understanding — that if they need it, it will be available to them. In the *Casey* decision, there is a healthy infusion of the idea that this has got to be the woman's choice.

JR: In your dissent in *Gonzales v. Carhart,* you criticized the Court for backing away from the equality principle recognized in *Casey.*

RBG: That was in a partial-birth abortion case. And there what concerned me about the Court's attitude, they were looking at the woman as not really an adult individual. The opinion said that the woman would live to regret her choice. That was not anything this Court should have thought or said. Adult women are able to make decisions about their own lives' course no less than men are. So, yes, I thought in *Carhart* the Court was *way* out of line. It was a new form of "Big Brother must protect the woman against her own weakness and immature misjudgment."

JR: You objected that the majority was being paternalistic in imagining that women needed protection from their own choices; they might regret their choices and have second thoughts.

RBG: Yes, the woman had to be protected from her own misjudgment. That she would, in time, understand that she had made a dreadful mistake. But adults make mistakes. They are adults. They're entitled to make judgments for themselves.

JR: And the opinion in *McCullen v. Coakley,* involving the First Amendment and abortion clinics, seemed to be unanimous, but you noted that some of these cases that look unanimous actually have deep divisions underlying them. Tell us about *McCullen.*

RBG: This was Massachusetts's attempt to deal with demonstrators at abortion clinics. The legislature passed a law that said, we want a thirty-five-foot buffer zone surrounding this clinic, and nobody can cross that line. The case was brought by women who called themselves counselors, and what they said is, we are not rock throwers, we're not shouters. We want to have a conversation with the women before they enter the clinic and tell them there's an alternative. But we can't get near them because of the thirty-five-foot buffer. The Court made one key ruling, and it was that the state can restrict speech when that speech endangers other people. So, for the boisterous demonstrators, the state of Massachusetts could take measures to protect the people who wanted access to the clinics. But Massachusetts had gone too far, because the record showed that some of the clinics never saw a demonstrator. The demonstrators came mostly to the clinic in Boston, and they came mostly on Saturdays. So the Court decided, yes, you can have restrictions to protect people's access, but you can't go so far that you are inhibiting people like the plaintiffs in that case. The instruction was, Massachusetts, rethink your law, come up with something that is less restrictive than this thirty-five-foot buffer zone every day in every place.

There was a strong disagreement on the Court about the first step — that is, could you have these laws aimed at people who were trying to impede access to the clinics? The Court said, yes, you could. The Court was divided on that question, which will be very important, because when a legislature passes a law to protect entrance into a clinic, as long as they do it reasonably, as long as they don't go overboard, it will be okay. That's the principal message of that case.

During an interview that followed Justice Anthony Kennedy's replacement by Justice Brett Kavanaugh, I asked Justice Ginsburg again if she thought Roe v. Wade *would be overturned.*

JR: When we last talked a year ago, you were skeptically hopeful that *Roe* would not be overturned.

RBG: I remain of that view. One reason I'm hopeful, think of the old chief [William H. Rehnquist]. When we were confronted with the question — "should *Miranda* be overruled?" — he saved it, even though I don't know how many times he'd criticized it. And if you compare Rehnquist's decision upholding the Family and Medical Leave Act, that certainly was not what you would expect from the justice who sat in the seventies. Roberts clerked for Rehnquist.

JR: Do you think Justice Kavanaugh would vote the same way as Kennedy?

RBG: Probably not on some controversy-generating issues.

JR: So, it's all up to the chief, as so much is, now that he's at the center of the Court.

RBG: Kavanaugh clerked for Kennedy, I think he did my very first year on the Court.

JR: What about these new fetal life laws, designed to challenge the heart of *Roe,* and declaring that life begins at the moment of conception?

RBG: Some states prohibit abortion when

a doctor can hear a fetal heartbeat. That can be around six weeks, when some women don't even know they're pregnant. But it all comes down to the same thing. Even in the worst case, if *Roe* is overruled, there's no woman of means who could not get a safe abortion someplace in the United States. There will be a core of states that will never go back to the days of unsafe, back alley abortions. So, poor women have no choice, women of means will be able to decide for themselves. Does that make sense as national policy?

4
THE BILL OF RIGHTS AND EQUAL PROTECTION

Ruth Bader Ginsburg's passion for civil rights and civil liberties was kindled when she was a college student at Cornell University. In 1950 and 1951, at the height of the McCarthy era, two Cornell professors received subpoenas to testify before the House Un-American Activities Committee for their alleged Communist sympathies. Ginsburg discussed the hearings with her government professor Robert E. Cushman, who asked her to serve as his research assistant; together they created a library exhibit on book burning throughout the ages, which included books that McCarthy and his sympathizers had identified as disloyal.[1] Ginsburg's respect for the role of lawyers in combating threats to civil liberties was further developed in Professor Milton Konvitz's course on American ideals, which explored the philosophical underpinnings of the Constitution. Konvitz had worked as an assistant to Thurgood Marshall at the NAACP Legal Defense Fund, focusing on police brutality cases. Cushman inspired Ginsburg to go to law school, where she would later adopt Marshall's litigation strategy as a model.

When I asked Ginsburg about her favorite majority opinions, it was hardly a surprise that she began with the Virginia Military Institute case from 1996. In earlier conversations, she had emphasized the importance of striking down VMI's all-male admissions policy; in her view, it represented the culmination of challenges to single-sex public schools that she had first launched in the 1970s, in a challenge to the all-male admissions policy of Central High School in Philadelphia.[2]

More striking was her affinity for another case decided the same year, one that, as she acknowledged, didn't get much attention. In *M.L.B. v. S.L.J.*, decided by a six-to-three vote, Ginsburg wrote the majority opinion striking down a Mississippi law that conditioned a woman's ability to appeal a court decree in a civil case terminating all her parental rights on her ability to pay a two-hundred-dollar administrative fee. In previous cases, the Court had said that the right of appeal in criminal cases involving fundamental rights couldn't be conditioned on the ability to pay a filing fee; Ginsburg concluded that civil "decrees forever terminating parental rights" are also "in the category of case in which the State may not 'bolt the door to equal justice.' " In response to Justice Clarence Thomas's dissent that her decision would "open the floodgate" to litigation, Ginsburg emphasized that "choices about marriage, family life, and the upbringing of children are among associational rights this Court has ranked as 'of basic importance in our society,' " and that "parental termination decrees are among the most severe forms of state action."[3] The case united Ginsburg's years of teaching civil procedure, which convinced her of the burdens that procedural filing requirements can impose on poor litigants, with her concern for the rights of the divorced mother who had been judged an unfit parent by a court without being afforded a meaningful opportunity to file an appeal.

On the U.S. Court of Appeals, Ginsburg had also distinguished herself as a strong civil libertarian in cases involving free speech and religious liberty. As a staunch advocate of the separation of church and state, she feared that religious exemptions from generally applicable criminal and civil laws would risk entangling religion and government and undermining antidiscrimination laws. For this reason, as a lower court judge, she ruled against a priest from the Ethiopian Zion Coptic Church who said the First Amendment should be construed to grant him a religious-use exemption from the federal ban on marijuana.[4] And she invoked the same principle in her dissenting opinion from the *Hobby Lobby* case, where the Supreme Court, by a five-to-four vote, granted the Hobby Lobby Corporation an exemption from having to comply with the Affordable Care Act's contraceptive coverage mandate because of the religious beliefs of its owners.

Still, Ginsburg supported reasonable accommodations for religiously motivated individuals, such as Sabbath observers, which she compared to reasonable accommodations for pregnant women. In 2015, just before the Court decided a case called *Young v. United Parcel Service,*[5] she signaled her belief, ultimately embraced by six justices, that the Pregnancy Discrimination Act of 1979 required United Parcel Service to accommodate a worker's inability to lift more than twenty pounds during her pregnancy. As Ginsburg suggested, Congress's decision to define pregnancy discrimination as a form of sex discrimination overruled a Supreme Court decision from five years earlier that had reached the opposite conclusion. In *Geduldig v. Aiello,* Justice Potter Stewart had written for the Court that California could compensate workers for all occupational disabilities except pregnancy without violating the Constitution's equal protection mandate. (*General Electric v. Gilbert,* a 1976 decision, reached the same conclusion under Title VII of the Civil Rights Act of 1964, which prohibits discrimination "on the basis of sex.") Rather than discriminating between men and women, Stewart held, the California law made a reasonable distinction between "pregnant women and nonpregnant persons."[6]

Congress's decision to recognize pregnancy discrimination as sex discrimination vindicated one of Ginsburg's long-standing convictions. After a Supreme Court decision in 1979 that reaffirmed the principle that only intentional discrimination against women could violate the Constitution, and therefore preferential hiring of veterans was not discriminatory even though it had the effect of excluding women, Ginsburg and Susan Deller Ross, a staff attorney at the ACLU, had written an op-ed in the *New York Times* calling on Congress to repudiate the Court's interpretation of Title VII as requiring intentional discrimination. They argued that Congress should legislate to prohibit unintentional discrimination as well, focusing on differential treatment of pregnant women in the workplace. "If it is not sex discrimination to exclude pregnant women from standard, fringe benefit programs," they wrote, "is it sex discrimination to fire pregnant women, refuse to hire them, force them to take long, unpaid leaves or strip them of seniority rights when they return to work?"[7] Congress promptly obliged by passing the Pregnancy Discrimination Act, which states explicitly that Title VII's ban on sex discrimination in the workplace includes discrimination on the basis of pregnancy.

By 1984, however, the consensus among feminists had disintegrated entirely. The catalyst for the split was a California law that gave pregnant women special maternity leaves. By this time, Ginsburg had become a federal judge, but the ACLU, relying on the theories she had developed, argued that the California law was inconsistent with the Pregnancy Discrimination Act's command that pregnant women "shall be treated the same" as other temporarily disabled workers. Rather than invalidating the special maternity leaves granted to women, the ACLU argued, the Court should extend the leaves to men — once again invoking Justice Harlan's opinion in the *Welsh* case that, in cases involving discriminatory laws, extension was a valid alternative to invalidation.

ACLU staff members who worked on the brief recall being "viciously attacked" by feminist organizations in California, who accused them of being antiwoman. These groups argued that special benefits for pregnant women are necessary, despite their violation of formal equality. Because most workplaces are designed with men in mind, they argued, women need to be treated differently to be treated equally.

In a 1986 speech, Ginsburg tacitly endorsed the ACLU's position, noting the "boomerang effect" of special pregnancy benefits for women, who would be less likely to be hired in the first place. She also pointed to a legislative alternative, the Family and Medical Leave Act, which creates child-rearing benefits that can be claimed by men or women.[8] But in a 1987 case, *California Federal Savings & Loan Association v. Guerra,* the Supreme Court upheld the California law, and the special treatment camp claimed vindication. Its leaders then seized on the victory to propose far more radical benefits for pregnant women.

The debate among feminists about pregnancy benefits has had dramatic implications for the legal status of the right to choose abortion itself. As Ginsburg noted in a 1986 article, "The characterization of pregnancy discrimination as sex discrimination, requires the comparative analysis of the equal protection model. Its emphasis is on what is not unique about the reproductive process of women." By contrast, the difference that feminists focus on is what is unique about childbirth. They advocate special treatment for pregnant women based on their premise that men and women are not "similarly situated" because of their reproductive differences. This was the same premise that Justice Stewart had invoked in his 1974 holding that discrimination against pregnant women is permissible.

That's why Ginsburg's insistence that discrimination on the basis of pregnancy is a form of discrimination on the basis of sex is so central to her search for alternatives to the right to privacy, which does not appear explicitly in the Constitution, as a firm legal basis for protecting women's reproductive rights. Ginsburg has been far more willing to enforce privacy rights for women when they can be tied to the text of the Constitution, such as the Fourth Amendment's prohibition against unreasonable searches and seizures.

JR: What is the opinion that you've written that you think has done the most to advance civil liberties?

RBG: Oh, Jeff, that's like asking which of my four grandchildren I prefer. There have been so many. Well, in the women's rights arena, the *VMI* case.

JR: Tell us what those initials stand for.

RBG: VMI, I think you know, is the Virginia Military Institute, a school supported by the state that excluded women. And the question was whether a state can maintain a facility offering tremendous benefits to one sex but not the other. Many people had questions about the VMI case, and they went like this: Well, why would a woman want to go to that school and expose herself to the ratline? My response was, "Well, I wouldn't. My daughter wouldn't. You, although you're a man, you wouldn't, either. But there are some women who are ready, willing, and able to undergo the rigors of VMI. Why shouldn't they have the opportunity?" It was a very satisfying decision for me.

As my husband put it, writing this opinion meant I won the *Vorchheimer* case twenty years later. Now, what was the *Vorchheimer* case? There were two schools for gifted children in Philadelphia. One was called Central High, and the other was called Girls High. I thought the names told the story. There was a young woman who wanted to go to Central because it had better science and math facilities, infinitely better playing fields, but that opportunity wasn't available to her, so she brought a suit saying that she was being denied the equal protection of the laws. She won in the court of first instance, the federal district court. She lost two-to-one on appeal. The case came to the Supreme Court, and the Supreme Court divided four-to-four. Now, when we do that, we are unable to render a judgment; we simply affirm the decision of the court below, and it has no precedential value for any other case. So the federal judges stood evenly divided in the Central High case. By the time we get to the Virginia Military Institute case, the decision was seven-to-one, and that to me was a sign of the change in that twenty-year period.

JR: Tell us about another of your favorite majority opinions.

RBG: There was a decision on the civil side that didn't get much press. It's called *M.L.B. v. S.L.J.* The Court's precedent was, if you are too poor to afford counsel or to afford a transcript in a felony case, the state must provide legal assistance for you. MLB was a woman who was in a proceeding to terminate her parental status. A social worker had said she was an unfit mother and therefore her child will be taken from her, she would be declared a nonparent. When she lost the case in the court of first instance, she wanted to appeal. But in order to appeal in that state, you had to have a transcript. MLB had a volunteer lawyer, but she didn't have the two hundred dollars that it took to buy a transcript. And so, the Supreme Court of the state said, sorry, we can't entertain your appeal. You haven't paid the fee for the transcript. That case went to the Supreme Court. And her argument is, I am being deprived of the most precious thing to me, the right to be a parent to my child. The argument against her was, you are in a civil proceeding. In criminal cases, if you are poor, the state will provide a lawyer, and they will provide whatever fees are necessary. But your case is civil. So it was the distinction between civil cases, you're on your own; criminal cases, you get a lawyer and expenses paid by the state. I think most women appreciate that the loss of one's child is more devastating than six months in jail, much more devastating.

It was technically a civil case, but I was able to persuade a majority of the Court that depriving a parent of parental status is as devastating as a criminal conviction. The Court decided that if she can't get an appeal without a transcript, then the state must provide the transcript at no cost to her. That was a departure from the rigid separation of criminal cases, on the one hand, with the right to counsel paid by the state and a transcript paid by the state, and civil cases, in which you do not have those rights. You must be able to pay. I thought *M.L.B.* was a significant case in that regard, getting the Court to think about the impact on a woman like MLB of being declared a nonparent.

JR: You've identified two of your favorite cases, *VMI* and *M.L.B.*, in which you persuaded your male colleagues to empathize with women who had suffered discrimination and injustice. But I love your dissents as much as your majority opinions, because you're on fire in these dissents. There was one of them, from 2003, *Smith v. Doe.* It was about the Alaskan sex offender registration database. The Court upheld its retroactive application to offenders convicted before the act passed. You pointed out in dissent that there is no possibility of rehabilitation: all the bad information about you is now online, but you don't get a chance to put up the good information and put yourself in context. What's your thought in a civil liberties case where you really have to side with the unpopular side in order to defend constitutional values?

RBG: Most of the great constitutional decisions were made in cases brought by people that you and I might not like to have as our best buddy or next-door neighbor — think of *Gideon v. Wainwright.* But if we don't protect the people we don't like, we're going to lose protections for ourselves. The Fourth Amendment doesn't say you can search the bad guys but not the good guys.

Think of the case involving the members of the Westboro Baptist Church [*Snyder v. Phelps* (2011)], who were against the United States' participation in the Iraq war. They decided that one way to show their opposition was to have demonstrations at the funerals of people who had been killed in service in Iraq, a really horrible thing to do. They were restricted to an area. They were not allowed to come anywhere near the church, but they could be seen by people who were taking that road to the church. The Court's decision was these people would have no right to disrupt the service, they had no right to block entrance into the church, but they do have a right of free speech. And as much as we may find their speech hateful, as long as they're not harming anyone, they have a right to speak. The government can't censor the speech we don't like.

You know, this is an issue that has been burning since the nation was new, and there was, at the time when the nation was just formed, a cartoon showing an American soldier carting off a British Tory to prison. The caption was, "Liberty of speech to those who speak the speech of liberty." The government can't tell us what's the right way to think, to speak, to write, and as long as we're not endangering others, that right must be respected. We can't have Big Brother Government telling us what's the right way to think and to speak and to write. So that was, I thought, a very important case. Every one of us thought that it was a most dreadful thing to do. But there have been a lot of people, dreadful speakers in the history of the United States, and because they were allowed to speak, all of us can feel more secure in our right to speak. Do you know the song "The House I Live In"?

JR: No.

RBG: I think Paul Robeson sang it. But, anyway, it says, "And the right to speak my mind out, that's America to me."

JR: Wow. That's great. That's really beautiful. And coming back to other civil liberties dissents, your *Hobby Lobby* dissent was something that you obviously felt very strongly about. Tell us about why you felt so strongly about that case.

RBG: The health care act has a list of medical services that must be provided to insured employees, and on that list was contraceptive services — essential, preventative care for the woman. Hobby Lobby's owners had a deeply held, totally genuine belief that using certain contraceptives was sinful. And so, they said, we won't provide that coverage. If Hobby Lobby had been a religious organization, if it had been a nonprofit serving a religious community — well, the question never would have come up because the people, the members, would all be part of the same religious community, and so the members would not even ask for access to contraception. But Hobby Lobby was in business for profit. It employed hundreds of women who did not share those religious beliefs. So, my point was, if you're going to employ people, a diverse workforce, you cannot force your beliefs on the people who work for you. If that's a choice you want to make, if you want to be in business, then you have to play by the rules that all other businesses play by, and you can't disadvantage the people who work for you based on your belief, which they do not share. That was essentially my position in the *Hobby Lobby* case.

JR: And are you concerned that the decision might be expanded to leave groups to claim exemptions from generally applicable discrimination laws?

RBG: Well, we will see. I said something like, the Court is entering a minefield. And I gave a couple of examples in the dissent.

One of the examples was a religious sect that had a deeply held belief that a woman must not work unless she has the permission of her father or her husband. Now, could an employer who is of that view say, "I know about Title VII, this antidiscrimination in employment law. But this is my religion, so I have to get an exemption from that law"? That was one example. There are many others.

One case that I had in the years I was on the DC Circuit was a case brought by the Ethiopian Zion Coptic Church that had a sacrament. Their sacrament was marijuana. Now, unlike the Native American Church and peyote, which is smoked only in the religious ceremony and very carefully guarded to see that no one leaves intoxicated . . . this sect, their sacrament was marijuana ingested all day, every day. So, they wanted an accommodation to their deeply held religious belief.

It's going to be interesting to see what will come to us as a result of the *Hobby Lobby* decision.

JR: Is there one case where you wish you had a do-over? A decision you regret or a position you wish you had articulated even more forcefully?

RBG: I would repeat the advice that Judge Edward Tamm gave me when I was a new judge on the DC Circuit. It goes like this: Work hard on each opinion, but once the case is decided, don't look back; go on to the next case and give it your all. It's not productive to worry about what's out and released, over and done. That's advice I now give to people new to the judging business.

JR: On the other hand, you don't want to be inflexible in the face of changing technologies. I found inspiring the unanimous decision in *Riley v. California,* the cell phone decision from last year where all nine of you agreed that for the cops to search a cell phone when they arrest someone and look at all the information on there was like the general warrants that sparked the American Revolution, because our lives are on our cell phones. How were you — I don't think you're especially tech savvy. I've known you a long time. What sort of apps do you have?

RBG: Well, you know, during the argument, people said, well, Supreme Court justices don't carry two cell phones. I do.

JR: You do? You have two?

RBG: Yes.

JR: A private one and a public one, which is very sensible, and we should all follow that.

RBG: No, one that I can work easily, and the other I can't. But the rule had been that anything, if you're arrested, anything in your pocket is fair game. So if you have a wallet or if you have a diary, and the police have probable cause to arrest you, they can take anything that's on your person. And so, the government urged, a cell phone that's carried in one's pocket is just like a wallet or just like a diary. Well, the Supreme Court was savvy enough to know that you can pack into that cell phone much more than, in the Founders' days, an office with file cabinets could contain. And so, the Court said, no, if . . . the police would like to search a cell phone, they have to do what is the main rule for searches and seizures, get a warrant. Go to an impartial magistrate and show good reasons for your need to inspect this cell phone.

JR: These tech cases are so fascinating and so important because, as you say, people live their lives on their cell phones, as you know as well. There was the case involving GPS tracking, the Global Positioning System case, *United States v. Jones,* where the Court held again, unanimously, although there were important differences in reasoning, that the cops can't put a GPS device on the bottom of a suspect's car and track his movements 24/7 for a month. And some people thought the argument was lost when the chief justice asked the first question — he said, is it the government's position that you could put a GPS device on the members of this Court and track our movements? And when the lawyer said yes, the case was over. That was based on the Fourth Amendment, not the right to privacy.

RBG: There is no right of privacy written into the Constitution. There is the Fourth Amendment, protecting people against unreasonable searches and seizures. But there is a notion, an important notion, of liberty — that we should have liberty to carry on with our lives without Big Brother Government looking over our shoulder. That idea has come from the guarantee, the due process guarantee of liberty, rather than an explicit right of privacy.

JR: Another civil liberties question that

often comes up is whether foreigners abroad or in the United States have the same right to privacy as U.S. citizens.

RBG: Well, I can give you two answers. One is: anyone who is within our borders, anyone has the right to due process and equal protection, because the Constitution speaks of persons. So let's find the Fourteenth Amendment. It says, ". . . nor shall any State deprive any person of life, liberty, or property, without due process of law; nor deny to any person within its jurisdiction the equal protection of the laws." The use of the word *person* means that any person is entitled to due process and the equal protection of the law.

It's also my firm conviction that the Constitution follows the flag. That is, wherever a U.S. representative acts, our Constitution is her guidebook. That view is not shared by the current majority, but I think someday it will.

There was a good illustration of that in a most unusual case back in the days when Germany was divided. Two people from East Germany hijacked a plane in Warsaw and brought it to West Berlin. Skyjacking is a crime, but it was embarrassing for the Germans, because in their view there was one Germany, not East or West, so if you live in the East you should have free access to the West. So the German authorities didn't know what to do with the case. The United States offered a helping hand. They said, left over from World War II is this U.S. court for Berlin. We'll revive it, and we'll send a U.S. district judge to preside over the trial. It will be tried under the German criminal code, but by a U.S. judge. The U.S. judge arrives, and the first thing he asks: "Where are these people? Do they have lawyers?" They didn't, but he made sure that they had excellent counsel. And then he said, "Well, now we need a jury pool." Jury pool? Germans don't use juries. And the judge said, I do. Wherever I am, wherever I exercise my power, by virtue of the Constitution, the rights guaranteed in the Constitution must be respected. The State Department was to no end disturbed at this notion. It was quite remarkable, they played by all the rules, the defendants got all the protections that they would have had if they were tried in a U.S. court. But they were tried in a court in Germany, and the governing law, the governing substantive law, was the German criminal code. The U.S. judge was a man who believed, as I do, that if you are a federal official, this Constitution is your guide whether you are acting at home or abroad.

JR: Great example. As you say, the majority of the Court has held otherwise, but individual judges have held that the Constitution follows the flag.

Let's talk now about religious liberty. What happens when minority faiths find themselves in conflict with general rules of applicability?

RBG: The accommodation to religious practices has come up, say, for Sabbath observers. If the employer is able to accommodate without disrupting the rest of the workforce, the employer must. But in the *Hobby Lobby* case, by accommodating to the owners' religious belief, the government would be depriving the workforce of the insurance Congress said they should have. It's the point that I made before — yes, accommodation, but not when your arm is hitting at the other fellow's nose. Yes, all kinds of reasonable accommodations can be made.

We're going to have a case a little later this term of a woman who worked for a courier service. She was a driver, and she delivered packages. Her doctor told her that, during her pregnancy, she should not lift weights over twenty pounds. Her co-workers were ready, willing, and able to help her and do the heavy lifting that she couldn't do, but the employer said no. I don't have to accommodate you. You're not disabled. I have to accommodate disabled people, but being pregnant is not a disability. So she was discharged, and when she was hired back after childbirth, she said, "Well, I want to get compensation for the time I was wrongfully discharged. You had an obligation to accommodate me." That's one of the cases that we will hear this term.

It comes up because, in the seventies, the Supreme Court decided a case about pregnancy and ruled that women can't complain about pregnancy as sex discrimination because discrimination on the basis of pregnancy is not discrimination on the basis of sex. That was a stunning thing for the Court to do. And Congress very quickly passed the Pregnancy Discrimination Act. . . . The law said discrimination on the basis of pregnancy is discrimination on the basis of sex. That is the law the woman in this case is invoking against the employer who discharged her because he wouldn't accommodate to her weightlifting restrictions during her pregnancy.

JR: I think I do need to close with this question: So, I have the great privilege of leading this magnificent institution, the National Constitution Center, created by Congress "to disseminate information about the Constitution on a nonpartisan basis." Is the possibility of nonpartisan constitutional adjudication an unrealistic ideal?

RBG: This fundamental instrument of our government is something that all Americans should know about — I went to China some years ago, and there was a story in the paper about "Justice Carries Constitution in Her Pocket." The Chinese reporter was very impressed with that, because in many places, you would have a Bill of Rights that's equivalent to ours, maybe much more extensive in its coverage, but it's aspirational. It isn't real law. The Constitution of the United States is our highest law, and it trumps any other law. A constitution that has that position — that's not just aspirational, and that has stayed with us. You know, there's an old joke about someone going into a French bookstore and asking for a copy of the French Constitution. The bookseller replies, "Sorry, we don't deal in periodical literature." Imagine this Constitution from 1787, it is still governing us.

5
SISTERS IN LAW

Ever since President Jimmy Carter appointed Ruth Bader Ginsburg to the DC Circuit in 1980, as part of his push to diversify the federal courts, she has been focused on the importance of increasing the number of women on the bench. During her investiture to the Supreme Court on August 10, 1993, she emphasized that "six of [President Bill Clinton's] total of fourteen federal bench nominees thus far are women," concluding, "In my lifetime, I expect that there will be among federal judicial nominees, based on the excellence of their qualifications, as many sisters- as brothers-in-law."[1]

She went on to note that Justice Sandra Day O'Connor, the first woman appointed to the U.S. Supreme Court, often quoted a Minnesota Supreme Court justice, Mary Jeanne Coyne, to the effect that women judges didn't decide cases differently than men because "a wise old man and a wise old woman reach the same conclusion." Ginsburg concurred. "I agree, but I also have no doubt that women, like persons of different groups and ethnic origins, contribute what a fine jurist, the late Fifth Circuit judge Alvin Rubin, described as 'a distinctive medley of views influenced by differences in biology, cultural impact, and life experience.' "[2] Indeed, during O'Connor's service, she and Ginsburg often voted together in cases involving sex discrimination, and four of their male colleagues became 26 percent more likely to side with sex discrimination plaintiffs than they had been before O'Connor's arrival.[3]

How did Ginsburg reconcile her insistence on the importance of diversity on the bench with her frequently repeated admonition that "generalizations about the way women or men are . . . cannot guide me reliably in making decisions about particular individuals"? She didn't believe that all female judges view cases the same way but insisted that, in the aggregate, a diverse federal bench will be richer "in appreciation [of] what is at stake and the impact of its judgments if all of its members are [not] cast from the same mold."[4] And the Supreme Court oral argument in the 2009 case *Saf-*

ford Unified School District v. Redding dramatically confirmed her point. The case involved a thirteen-year-old middle school student, Samantha Redding, who endured a strip search of her bra and underwear as school officials looked in vain for prescription-strength painkillers. At the oral argument, Justice Stephen Breyer awkwardly asked what the big deal was. "Why is this a major thing to say strip down to your underclothes, which children do when they change for gym?" he observed, adding that when he was "eight or ten or twelve years old, you know, we did take our clothes off once a day, we changed for gym, and people did sometimes stick things in my underwear." After uncomfortable laughter in the courtroom, Ginsburg, then the only woman on the Court, added a woman's perspective to the exchange. "It wasn't just that they were stripped to their underwear!" she objected. "They were asked to shake their bra out, to stretch the top of their pants and shake that out!"[5] In his opinion for the Court, Justice David Souter, influenced by Ginsburg's insistence on viewing the search from Redding's perspective, noted her account of it as "embarrassing, frightening, and humiliating." Ginsburg added that it was "abusive."[6]

When Justice Ginsburg joined the Supreme Court, she greatly appreciated Sandra Day O'Connor's warm welcome. She called O'Connor "the most helpful big sister anyone could have," and one of her former clerks told the biographer Jane Sherron De Hart that Ginsburg considered her relationship with O'Connor more important than that with any other justice.[7] In presenting an award to O'Connor in 1997, Ginsburg recalled that when she received her first opinion assignment in October 1993, she expected to be given an easy one, producing a unanimous result, as is generally the case for a new justice. "When the list came around, I was dismayed," Ginsburg recalled. "I was assigned an intricate, not at all easy case, on which the Court sharply divided. I sought Sandra's advice. It was simple. 'Just do it,' she said, 'and if you can, get your draft in circulation before the next set of assignments is made.' " In the end, O'Connor dissented from Ginsburg's first majority opinion. But when Ginsburg read a summary of the opinion from the bench, O'Connor passed her a note. "This is your first opinion for the Court," the note read. "It is a fine one. I look forward to many more."[8]

Ginsburg appreciated O'Connor's commitment to civil dialogue, to disagreeing without being disagreeable. This commitment was in marked contrast to her friend Justice Antonin Scalia, whose barbed dissent claiming that one of O'Connor's opinions "cannot be taken seriously" prompted O'Connor to reply, "Sticks and stones can break my bones, but words will never hurt me." (She then added, "That probably isn't true.")[9] As Ginsburg put it, O'Connor "presents her disagreement plainly and professionally; she does not waste words castigating colleagues for 'terminal silliness,' or for their 'shocking,' 'profoundly misguided,' or 'simply irresponsible' views. (I am making none of those up.) In that respect, too, I am following her lead."[10]

Often asked whether the Court had turned around after the arrival of two women, Ginsburg replied, "Our robing room, since the 1993 term, has a women's bathroom equal in size to the men's." It took Ginsburg's arrival, twelve years after O'Connor's, to persuade the justices to install a women's bathroom adjacent to the robing room.

In 2009, sixteen years after Ginsburg's nomination and three years after O'Connor's retirement, Sonia Sotomayor was confirmed as the third woman to serve on the Supreme Court, followed the next year by Elena Kagan. Ginsburg welcomed the arrival of her fellow New Yorkers. Kagan first met Ginsburg while clerking for Abner Mikva, the judge on the U.S. Court of Appeals for the DC Circuit for whom I also clerked. "She has already gained applause for her incisive questioning at oral argument and crisp writing," Ginsburg told the Second Circuit judicial conference at the end of Kagan's first term on the Supreme Court. And she repeatedly expressed the hope that more women would follow, suggesting that there would be enough women on the Court "when there were nine."[11]

Her relationship with O'Connor remained close during the thirteen years they served together. They agreed in only 52 percent of the nonunanimous cases,[12] and some of the disagreements, such as *Bush v. Gore,* were significant. But O'Connor was always respectful of Ginsburg's trailblazing achievements for gender equality. O'Connor declined Justice John Paul Stevens's attempt to assign her the Virginia Military Institute case striking down single-sex public education for men only, insisting that "this should be Ruth's."[13]

In the summer of 2005, when O'Connor announced her decision to retire to care for her husband, whose Alzheimer's disease was quickly progressing, Ginsburg mourned the loss of her friend on the bench as well as the death that same year of Chief Justice William Rehnquist, whose sense of humor and courage in struggling with thyroid cancer Ginsburg had much admired. As the Court turned to the right in 2006, following the appointments of Justice Samuel Alito and Chief Justice John Roberts, Ginsburg felt isolated as the only woman on an increasingly conservative Court. She began to recast herself from the moderate minimalist to the notorious dissenter and, during this transition, redoubled her long-standing workout routines derived from the Royal Canadian Air Force exercises, which she described to me in detail.

In 1999, after recovering from colorectal cancer, Ginsburg had begun working out with Bryant Johnson, a paratrooper and personal trainer whose day job was in the District Court clerk's office. ("You look like an Auschwitz survivor. You must get a personal trainer to regain strength and well-being," Marty had told Ruth after the successful chemotherapy.)[14] She continued to work out with Johnson (except during his deployment to Kuwait from 2004 to 2007), and in 2017, Johnson published their routine in a book called *The RBG Workout.*

After years of hour-long workouts twice a week in the Supreme Court gym, Ginsburg's bone density increased and, with her iron focus and determination, she graduated from doing push-ups against a wall to what Johnson called "full-on standard push-ups the way I learned to do them in basic training for the Army." Ginsburg's determination and focus inspired Johnson's mother to lose fifty pounds and to exercise regularly, just as they have inspired other men and women, younger and older, to take up disciplined weight and cardio training. And, in the process, Ginsburg has become one of the fittest members of the Supreme Court. During a conversation at George Washington University in 2018, she was asked which of her fellow justices could do more push-ups. "Maybe Justice Neil Gorsuch," she replied, noting that her fifty-one-year-old colleague rides a bike to work every day. "I think our chief is also a possibility."[15]

JR: Justice Ginsburg — three women on the Court. Justice O'Connor was the first, then there were two, then there was one again, now two, and finally three. How do you feel? Should there be more?

RBG: There will be. You know, I have said,

"I expect in my lifetime to see three, four, maybe more women on the U.S. Supreme Court." We are a little bit behind Canada. Canada has nine justices; four of them are women, including their chief justice. But we will get there.

JR: You've known Elena Kagan for a while, I think. How did you meet her?

RBG: I met her first when she was clerking for Ab Mikva, and then I next got to know Elena, or she got to know me, when I was nominated by President Clinton, when Joe Biden was the chairman of the Senate Judiciary Committee. He wanted to be well prepared for the hearing, so he borrowed Elena, who was then working at the White House, and he asked her to read every opinion I ever wrote, every speech I ever gave, so she could inform him and suggest questions to ask me at the hearing. So Elena knew me quite well. When she became solicitor general, I lost my best law clerk picker, because I had an arrangement with Elena when she was the dean of the Harvard Law School that she would pick one of my four law clerks each term, and I have been exceedingly well served by the law clerks she chose.

JR: What was she like as solicitor general?

RBG: Her very first court, the very first court Elena ever argued before, was the U.S. Supreme Court, and she was superb. She was a wonderful advocate in every argument she gave. She had a bit of a problem [when she was nominated to the Supreme Court in 2010], because she had written about my nomination and Steve Breyer's nomination, and said she wished we had been a little more revealing than we were. Older and wiser, she steered the same course we did.

JR: How did she do? Do you think she steered it well?

RBG: I thought she was terrific. I wrote her a note saying, "It takes two qualities, and that's all you need to know. One is patience, and the other is a sense of humor." I think she showed both.

JR: People are curious, of course, about the dynamics on this remarkable body. I think from my parochial perspective of an endless faculty meeting, where you're locked in a room with the same nine people for a very long time. How do you get along?

RBG: Of all the places I've worked, all the law faculties I've been a member of, there is no workplace that I've found more collegial than the U.S. Supreme Court. We are, in a real sense, a family, no matter how strongly we disagree on important questions, and we do, we genuinely respect, like, and care about one another. When I had my first bout with cancer, colorectal cancer, in 1999, Sandra's advice to me when I had to have chemotherapy was, "Do it on Friday, and you'll get over it on the weekend and be able to come back to work on Monday." The other thing she told me, and I was so glad to follow her advice, she said, "You're going to get letters from all over the country — people will be wishing you well. Don't even try to respond."

My favorite story from the first cancer bout was, my dear colleague David Souter, along with all my other colleagues, he said, "Ruth, if there's anything, anything in the world I can do to help you get through this time, just call on me." One afternoon, one Friday afternoon, I got a call from Marty saying, "When you get finished with the chemo, then please come to see me. I'm in the cardiac wing of Washington Hospital Center." It was nothing life-threatening, but he had to be there two nights. And I had tickets to the Washington National Opera the next evening. So I called David Souter and said, "David, you said anything, anything at all. I don't want to sit next to an empty seat tomorrow night. Will you join me?" Now, this audience won't appreciate what a tremendous feat that was, to get David to come to the Kennedy Center. He had been invited dozens and dozens of times, and except for an event honoring Justice Thurgood Marshall, he ever so politely declined. He enjoyed the opera enormously, but he never came back of his own accord.

JR: How has the dynamic on the Court changed as it has added more women?

RBG: Justice O'Connor and I were together for more than twelve years, and in every one of those twelve years, sooner or later, at oral argument, one lawyer or another would call me Justice O'Connor. They were accustomed to the idea that there was a woman on the Supreme Court and her name was Justice O'Connor. Sandra would often correct the attorney; she would say, "I'm Justice O'Connor, she's Justice Ginsburg." The worst times were the years I was alone. The image to the public entering the courtroom was eight men, of a certain size, and then this little woman sitting to the side. That was not a good image for the public to see. But now, with the three of us on the bench, I am no longer lonely, and my newest colleagues are not shrinking violets. Justice Sotomayor even beat out Justice Scalia as the justice who asked the most questions during argument.

JR: Is it a good thing that women are galvanized to run for office? What would you tell those who are hesitating in trying to decide whether to run?

RBG: I think the women today have a lot more support than they once did from groups campaigning for them. Well, think even of our Court: Sandra Day O'Connor was appointed in 1981, and there had never been a woman before. When I was appointed to the DC Circuit by Jimmy Carter — Jimmy Carter was a man who changed, literally changed, the complexion of the U.S. judiciary. He wasn't a lawyer himself. He looked around at the federal judiciary and observed, "They all look just like me, just like me. They are all white men. But that is not how the great United States looks. I want my judges to be drawn from all of the people, not just some of them."

So he made an effort to appoint minority group members and women, not one at a time, but in numbers. He appointed, I think, more than twenty-five women to the federal trial court, the federal district courts. He appointed eleven to courts of appeals, and I was one of the lucky eleven. So, when people ask, did you always want to be a judge? I smile and say, when I graduated from law school, there were no women on the federal appellate bench. There had been Florence Allen, who was appointed in 1934 by President Roosevelt, and she retired in 1959, and so then there were none. There were none until Shirley Hufstedler was appointed by President Johnson to the Court of Appeals for the Ninth Circuit. And then Jimmy Carter became president and set a pattern that no president has departed from. President Reagan, not to be outdone, was determined to appoint the first woman to the Supreme Court. He made a nationwide search and came up with a splendid candidate, Sandra Day O'Connor.

Nowadays, there are three of us, one-third of the bench, and because of my seniority, I sit close to the middle. Justice Sotomayor is near one end, Justice Kagan near the other, and they are very active in the colloquy that goes on in argument.

JR: You were interested in that survey that found that the women justices were interrupted more. What is your considered judgment of that?

RBG: I think my colleagues would notice that and perhaps be more careful. But we all — we do interrupt each other, as the former law clerks here know. One of the most amusing incidents of that — there was an oral argument and Justice O'Connor, who often asked the first question, had paused, and I thought she was done, so I asked a question. She said, "Just a minute. I'm not finished." I apologized to her at lunch. She said, "Ruth, don't give it another thought. The guys do it to each other all the time."

The next day in *USA Today* is a headline: RUDE RUTH INTERRUPTS SANDRA. I was asked to comment, so I said what Sandra had said at lunch, the men interrupt each other regularly, and you haven't noticed that. That reporter, to his credit, watched the Court through the next two sittings and said, "You know, you're right, I just never noticed it when it was two men." Then an academic whose specialty was language wrote an op-ed piece in the *Washington Post* to explain how this happened, how I interrupted Sandra. She said, "Well, Justice Ginsburg is a Jew who grew up in New York City, and those people talk fast. Justice O'Connor is a girl of the Golden West, laid-back, speaks slowly."

People who knew the two of us recognized immediately that Sandra got out two words to my every one, but it is a wonderful example of the stereotype.

JR: You have a very different style on the bench and in conversation. On the bench, you are right in there, but in conversation, all your friends know it is in the pauses we have to wait, because you are about to say something very special.

RBG: [long pause]

[laughter]

Yes, my law clerks know that, too.

[laughter]

Well, I try to think before I speak.

[laughter]

It is something my husband learned as a law teacher. He was concerned that the men were volunteering much more often than the women, and one of his colleagues gave him advice. She said, "Don't ever call on the first hand that is raised; that will invariably be a man. Wait five, six seconds, and you will see women's hands go up, because women were thinking before they spoke."

JR: Why is it good for men — you've said that there should be nine women on the Supreme Court.

RBG: No, I didn't say there should be. The question was when will there be enough, so there'll be enough when there are nine.

For most of our history, except the times the Court was less than nine, and the one time there were ten, they were, until Justice O'Connor, all men. And nobody thought anything was unusual about that.

JR: But you weren't joking. And would it be good for men and women to have nine women?

RBG: We've had state supreme courts with all women. I think Minnesota did for a while. We've had many states that had a majority women.

JR: And why is it good? Is it because, as you say so powerfully, generalizations about the way men and women are can't guide you in particular cases, and therefore it shouldn't matter whether there are nine women or five women?

RBG: There is a life experience that women have that brings something to the table. I think a collegial body is much better off to have diverse people of different backgrounds and experience that can make our discussions more informed.

In one case it was evident a thirteen-year-old girl was suspected of having the wrong kind of pills in school. She was taken to the girls' restroom and strip-searched. The pills she had in her purse — I think there was one Advil and one aspirin. After she was strip-searched and no contraband found, she was put in a chair in front of the principal's office, and her mother was called to take her home.

Her mother was, let's say, beside herself that her daughter had been humiliated in that way, so she brought a suit under a post–Civil War antidiscrimination law — we call it a Section 1983 suit. The oral argument took a light tone. One of my colleagues said the boys undress in front of each other in the locker room, and there is nothing embarrassing about that. My response was that a thirteen-year-old girl is not like a thirteen-year-old boy in that regard. It's a difficult stage in her growing up, and there were suddenly no more jokes.

I guess my colleagues were thinking of their wives and daughters. But that kind of insight I have because I have grown up female. So it's not that women decide cases differently than men — they don't. A woman who served on the Supreme Court of Minnesota, Jeanne Coyne, said at the end of the day a wise old man and a wise old woman will reach the same judgment. But nevertheless, she said, we bring something to the table that was absent when the judiciary was all male.

JR: What decisions would have come out differently if Justice O'Connor were still on the Court?

RBG: She would have been with us in *Citizens United,* in *Shelby County,* probably in *Hobby Lobby,* too.

JR: Do you think she regrets her decision to retire?

RBG: She made a decision long ago to retire at age seventy-five. She thought she and her husband, John, would be able to do all the outdoorsy things they liked to do. When John's Alzheimer's disease made those plans impossible, she had already announced her retirement. I think she must be concerned about some of the Court's rulings, those that veer away from opinions she wrote.

JR: Speaking of retirements, there are some who say that you should have stepped down earlier, when the political landscape was more favorable to the Democrats. How do those suggestions make you feel, and what's your response?

RBG: First, I should say, I am fantastically lucky that I am in a system without a compulsory retirement age. Most countries of the world have as mandatory retirement ages sixty-five, seventy, seventy-five, and many of our states do as well. As long as I can do the job full steam, I will stay here. I think I will know when I'm no longer able to think as lucidly, to remember as well, to write as fast. I was number one last term in the speed with which opinions came down. My average from the day of argument to the day the decision was released was sixty days, ahead of the chief by some six days. So I don't think I have reached the point where I can't do the job as well.

I asked some people, particularly the academics who said I should have stepped down when President Obama was in office: "Who do you think the president could nominate and get through the current Senate that you would rather see on the Court than me?" No one has given me an answer to that question.

JR: Your health is good?

RBG: Yes, and I'm still working out twice a week with my trainer, the same trainer I now share with Justice Kagan. I have done that since 1999.

JR: Do you work out together?

RBG: No, she's a lot younger than I am, younger than my daughter. She does boxing, a great way to take out your frustrations.

JR: And what do you do?

RBG: I do a variety of weightlifting, elliptical glider, stretching exercises, push-ups. And I do the Canadian Air Force exercises almost every day.

JR: Are those the exercises you did when I met you at the Court of Appeals in 1991?

RBG: No. I was part of a Jazzercise class. It was an aerobics routine accompanied by loud music, sounding quite awful to me. Jazzercise was popular in the eighties and nineties.

JR: What are the Canadian Air Force exercises?

RBG: They were published in a paperback book put out by the Canadian Air Force. When I was twenty-nine, that exercise guide was very popular. I was with Marty at a tax conference in Syracuse. We stopped to pick up a lawyer to attend the morning program with us. He said, "Just a moment, I have to finish my exercises." I asked him what those exercises were. He replied they were the Canadian Air Force exercises and said he wouldn't let a day go by without doing them.

The lawyer who told me about the Canadian Air Force exercises stopped doing them years ago. I still do the warm-up and stretching regime almost every day.

6
NINO

In 1993, as President Clinton was deliberat-
ing on his choice for the Supreme Court, I
attended a brown bag lunch with the law
clerks at the U.S. Court of Appeals in
Washington. They told me that, at a similar
lunch months earlier, someone asked Justice
Antonin Scalia, "If you had to spend the
rest of your life on a desert island with Lau-
rence Tribe or Mario Cuomo, which would
you choose?" His reply, without missing a
beat: "Ruth Bader Ginsburg." I reported
the story in the *New Republic* piece endors-
ing Ginsburg, and she recalled it at Justice
Scalia's memorial service in Washington in
May 2016, adding that "within days, the
president chose me."[1]

There's no doubt that the respect that
Justice Scalia and other conservatives held
for Ginsburg during her twelve years on the
U.S. Court of Appeals was a factor in
Clinton's decision. "Ruth Bader Ginsburg

cannot be called a liberal or a conservative," Clinton said when he nominated her. "She has proved herself too thoughtful for such labels."[2] Scalia and Ginsburg's mutual respect and affection, however, were rooted not in ideological affinity but in a shared love of music and a sense of humor. "He was a jurist of captivating brilliance and wit, with a rare talent to make even the most sober judge laugh,"[3] Ginsburg wrote in a moving tribute days after his death.

In her eulogy, she told other stories about how humor allowed the two friends to disagree over the years with relative equanimity. "Once asked how we could be friends, given our disagreement on lots of things, Justice Scalia answered: 'I attack ideas. I don't attack people. Some very good people have some very bad ideas,'" Ginsburg recalled, to laughter. "In his preface to the libretto of the opera *Scalia/Ginsburg,* Justice Scalia described as the peak of his days in DC an evening in 2009 at the Opera Ball at the British Ambassador's Residence, when he joined two National Opera tenors at the piano for a medley of songs. He called it the famous Three Tenors performance."[4]

Ginsburg, even more than Scalia, loved the opera *Scalia/Ginsburg,* written by Derrick Wang, then a University of Maryland law school student. When the National Constitution Center staged a concert performance of the opera in Washington, DC, in 2014, I had the special pleasure of playing Name That Tune with Ginsburg as we both identified the quotations from favorite composers that Wang used to set the various arias, including Handel, Mozart, Strauss, Bizet, and Gilbert and Sullivan. Ginsburg's favorite aria was the duet "We Are Different, We Are One," a hymn to their bipartisan friendship and love for the Constitution.

We are different.
We are one.
The U.S. contradiction.

The tension we adore.

Sep'rate strands unite in friction.
To protect our country's core.
This the strength of our nation.
Thus is our Court's design.
We are kindred.
We are nine.

When this kinship, and the Court's bipartisan legitimacy, seemed threatened after the polarizing confirmation hearings of

140

Brett Kavanaugh in September 2018, Ginsburg criticized the party-line votes into which confirmation hearings had deteriorated. And she contrasted the Kavanaugh hearings, where the nominee received no Democratic votes, with the confirmation hearings that she and Justice Scalia experienced, where the votes were nearly unanimous. "The way it was was right. The way it is is wrong," she told an interviewer at George Washington University.[5]

Ginsburg and Scalia voted together far less frequently in their final years on the Court than they did in Ginsburg's first year, where scholars found "no single ideological alignment" in her voting patterns.[6] But they remained close because of the strength of their friendship, sustained by gourmet meals cooked by Marty Ginsburg and culminating in an annual New Year's Eve dinner at the Ginsburgs' home that often involved singing together around the piano. Marty became close to Scalia's wife, Maureen, who wrote the introduction to *Chef Supreme,* a collection of his recipes published in his memory in 2011 by "the associate spouses" of the justices. As Maureen Scalia put it, "It wasn't simply that Marty was the Supreme Chef, it was the enthusiasm with which he approached the creation of a meal, his lovely small smile as he watched all of us enjoy his work, and his kind patience with us in turn." She continued: "I could plan, and execute my part of our menu, and see that smile encouraging me. But not when I suggested that bread be bought, and by me. This, to Marty, was just not possible, not thinkable. A very sad thought, a very sad look, and then 'I'll take care of the bread.' "

Ginsburg never concealed her strong disagreement with what she viewed as Scalia's activist jurisprudence. She often dissented from cases where he was in the majority, from *Bush v. Gore* in 2000 to *District of Columbia v. Heller* in 2008, which recognized an individual Second Amendment right to bear arms. Still, even after *Bush v. Gore,* she and Scalia remained close. As she recalled at his memorial service:

Another indelible memory, the day the Court decided *Bush v. Gore,* December 12, 2000. I was in chambers, exhausted after the marathon: review granted Saturday, briefs filed Sunday, oral argument Monday, and opinions completed and released Tuesday. No surprise, Justice Scalia and I were on opposite sides.

The Court did the right thing, he had no doubt. I disagreed and explained why in a dissenting opinion. Around 9:00 p.m. the telephone, my direct line, rang. It was Justice Scalia. He didn't say, "Get over it." Instead, he asked, "Ruth, why are you still at the Court? Go home and take a hot bath." Good advice I promptly followed.[7]

Scalia consoled Ginsburg after Marty's death, and she was distraught by Scalia's sudden passing in February 2016. Three years older than Scalia, she couldn't help but think when she heard the news, "I was supposed to go first."[8]

JR: You and I met over opera. It was almost twenty-five years ago, and I was a law clerk on the U.S. Court of Appeals and you were a judge. I couldn't think of what to say to this incredibly intimidating and impressive woman, so I just started chatting about the one thing that I really love, and that is opera. And it turned out that you liked it a whole lot, too, and we very quickly built up a friendship over the years, bonding over opera and talking about it in all its dimensions. And I could never have imagined, when we first met, that it would have culminated in watching a spectacular performance of *Scalia/Ginsburg* together. I had no idea it was so good!

RBG: Oh, you didn't hear my greatest aria. In one of the major scenes that was left out, I break through the glass ceiling to rescue Justice Scalia as the Queen of the Night, from *The Magic Flute.*

JR: How do you rescue him?

RBG: By doing a lot of singing. I think we wear the Commentator's patience.

JR: It essentially tells the story of how these two people with very different personalities — one bombastic, and the other quite demure — are locked in a room at the Supreme Court and the only way to get out is to agree to a common approach on the Constitution.

RBG: We agree to be different.

JR: You agree to be different. That line at the end, "We are different, we are one." First of all, it's incredibly moving, the idea that in a country so driven by partisanship and polarization, people can strongly disagree about the Constitution but still be united by the Constitution. Is that a realistic hope?

RBG: I think it is. It was for me, and it was for Justice Scalia. When he was nominated, although his views were very well known, he was confirmed unanimously. And I came pretty close to that — the vote on me was ninety-six to three. It would not be that way today, but don't you think that's the direction in which we should seek to return?

JR: Yes, enthusiastically, everyone says yes. How can we seek to return there? How can we explain the fact that you had this friendship, and although you disagreed constitutionally, you were united by a love for the Constitution?

RBG: I think that, as Derrick Wang captured it so well, we do revere the Constitution and the institution of the Court.

JR: Everyone wants to know, of course, how could you be friends given the fact that you disagree?

RBG: We were colleagues on the Court of Appeals. And one thing about Justice Scalia — he was a very funny man. Now, every year, they rate the justices on how many laughs we produce at argument, and Scalia was always number one, and I am always number nine. But sometimes, he could say things and just . . . I had to pinch myself to stop laughing.

JR: And you also shared this love of opera, and you spent New Year's together?

RBG: Yes.

JR: What did he think of *Scalia/Ginsburg*?

RBG: When Derrick first came to him and said, "Do you mind if I do this?" his answer was, "You have a First Amendment right to do this."

JR: And after seeing it?

RBG: I think he enjoyed it very much, and particularly the tribute to his father in the aria about building stairs. And you should appreciate that every line in the libretto is footnoted with references to opinions, to articles. So, it's staggering, the job [Derrick Wang] did.

JR: It is staggering. And he wrote all the lyrics, too. What are some of your favorite lines?

146

RBG: I like the one about the Constitution . . . Like our society, it can evolve.

JR: It's magnificent, and I never knew that anyone could find a rhyme for *Craig v. Boren* before. It's very well done. You sing:

> The cases we'd select,
> Though sometimes indirect,
> Would have a grand effect
> The thirsty boys and Whitener's store in
> The case of *Craig v. Boren*.

RBG: Well, a lot of those references may be hard to grasp. That's why the footnoted version of the libretto should be published. Those were all cases that came before the Court in the 1970s.

JR: Now, sometimes the rhetoric can be quite strong, and you're telling us that it's really not personal. I was especially moved, as many people were, by your passionate dissent in the *Carhart* case, the partial-birth abortion case. You objected to the gender stereotypes that were inherent in the idea that women had to be protected from their bad decisions. Was it difficult to challenge a colleague that directly? You seemed to really care about that case, and it seemed to go against much of your legacy.

RBG: Yes, but I did not say about the other side, "This opinion is profoundly misguided" or "This opinion is not to be taken seriously."

JR: These are Justice Scalia's words.

RBG: Yes.

JR: He said that about one of Justice O'Connor's opinions, and she very calmly said, "Sticks and stones will break my bones," which was an excellent retort.

RBG: I never saw that kind of invective in any Sandra Day O'Connor opinion. They are distracting asides, so I don't use them.

JR: How did *Scalia/Ginsburg* come about?

RBG: Derrick Wang, the writer, librettist, composer, is a delightful young man. He was a music major at Harvard, he has a master's in music from Yale, and then he decided he should know a little bit about the law. He's from Baltimore, and he enrolled in the University of Maryland Law School. And in his second year, he took

Constitutional Law, and read opinions by Justice Scalia, opinions by me, sometimes for the Court, sometimes in dissent, and he thought he could make a very funny opera about our divergent views. So that's how it all started.

JR: *Scalia/Ginsburg* sounds like one of the great buddy movies of all time.

RBG: Well, it's roughly based on *The Magic Flute.* Justice Scalia has to go through certain trials, and he's not able to do it on his own, so I come along and make it possible for him to succeed. Perhaps if I recited the first words of Justice Scalia's opening aria, you'll get the idea.

JR: That would be great. Please do that.

RBG: It's his rage aria, and it goes this way: "The justices are blind! / How can they possibly spout this? / The Constitution says absolutely nothing about this."

JR: The man clearly has talent. I got from the NPR excerpt, from the libretto, a similarly inspired line set to the music of "The Star-Spangled Banner": "Oh Ruth, can you read? You're aware of the text. / Yet so proudly you've failed to derive its true meaning."

I remember years ago when I was talking to law clerks before you were nominated to the bench; they had just heard Justice Scalia asked the question, "If you were locked on a desert island, who would you like it to be with?" And he said that it would be Ruth Bader Ginsburg.

RBG: Well, there wasn't much competition.

JR: And you became dear friends, despite your serious constitutional disagreements. How was it possible to maintain this personal friendship when the two of you were engaged in intellectual and constitutional conflict?

RBG: I should say that one of the hallmarks of the Court is collegiality, and we could not do the job that the Constitution gives to us if we didn't, to use one of Scalia's favorite expressions, "Get over it." We know that even though we have sharp disagreements on what the Constitution means, we have a trust. We revere the Constitution and the Court, and we want to make sure that when we leave it, it will be in as good shape as it was when we joined the Court. There were a number of cases that —

they're not picked up by the press too often — where Justice Scalia and I were in total agreement. I think of a Fourth Amendment case [*Maryland v. King*] where Nino was in dissent. The question was whether the police, when they arrest someone suspected of a felony, whether they can take a DNA sample. The majority said DNA today is just like fingerprints yesterday. Scalia's dissent was: DNA is marvelously effective in solving unsolved crimes, but to pretend it is being used to identify the arrestee — the arrestee has already been arraigned, so we know who the arrestee is. It is being used to find out whether this person committed some yet-unsolved crime. And that's all very well and good, except that our Constitution says that we are not to be subjected to unreasonable searches. That the normal rule is: if the police suspect a person of committing a crime, the police goes to a magistrate, presents probable cause for believing this person committed a crime, and gets a warrant. Well, that's what's missing when you take a DNA sample, run it through a computer, and find that this person has committed — in the case we had, it was a horrendous rape.

JR: I thought that was one of Justice Scalia's

most inspiring dissents. It was hugely important. He had that great line about how "the proud men who wrote the charter of our liberties" would have refused to "open their mouths for royal inspection," and it's a very important reminder of the necessity of warrants before collecting information on people without suspicion.

Justice Scalia in the opera sings a lot of Puccini. And I love the fact that your character in *Scalia/Ginsburg* first appears to the music of *Carmen.*

RBG: I like the last duet, "We Are Different, We Are One." The idea is that there are two people who interpret the Constitution differently yet retain their fondness for each other and, much more than that, their reverence for the institution that employs them.

7
THE TWO CHIEFS

During her first twelve years on the Supreme Court, Justice Ginsburg served with Chief Justice William Rehnquist. She referred to him as "my chief" and was especially fond of him. "Of all the bosses I have had as lawyer, law teacher, and judge, Chief Justice William Hubbs Rehnquist was hands down the fairest and most efficient," she wrote in a tribute after his death in 2005. "He kept us all in line and on time."[1]

What was it that drew the civil libertarian from New York to the libertarian conservative from Arizona? Part of the appeal, as Ginsburg suggested, was her respect for Rehnquist's no-nonsense efficiency and sense of fairness in assigning Supreme Court opinions. (When the chief justice is in the majority, he has the power to decide which justice writes the opinion of the Court.) Ginsburg appreciated that Rehnquist assigned the most interesting cases on the basis not of ideology but of which justices had completed their previous assignments on time. When Ginsburg joined the Court, O'Connor warned her that if she failed to circulate the draft of her first opinion before Rehnquist made the next set of assignments, "you will risk receiving another tedious case."[2] That's because Rehnquist, who set ten-day deadlines for himself in producing the first drafts of majority opinions, was similarly exacting when it came to his colleagues: he would punish justices who fell behind on their opinion writing (such as the famously slow Harry Blackmun) by not assigning them new ones, or by giving them the least desirable leftovers. Ginsburg, who is similarly strict about meeting and enforcing deadlines, took the advice to heart and worked to turn in what she called her homework assignments (that is, the drafts of her majority opinions) more quickly than any other justice. She also appreciated the speed with which Rehnquist ran the justices' private, twice-weekly conferences. He would briskly go around the table in order of seniority, asking each justice to state his or her views, without allowing the discussions to wander. Some justices complained that this discouraged deliberation, but it appealed to Ginsburg, who likes to use every moment efficiently, for focused and productive work.[3]

In addition to Rehnquist's efficiency and fairness in assigning opinions, Ginsburg appreciated his thoughtfulness and "humane qualities" during her recovery from colorectal cancer surgery in 1999. "He kept my assignments light during the most trying weeks and let me decide when I could tackle more challenging cases. Coping with cancer himself last term, his courage and determination were exemplary, inspiring others battling debilitating diseases to carry on with their lives and work as best they can," she wrote in his memorial tribute. And she enjoyed Rehnquist's "poker face" sense of humor, noting that when a reporter asked him in 1986 whether his appointment as chief justice was the culmination of a dream, he replied, "I wouldn't call it [that], but it's not every day when you're 61 years old that you get a chance to have a new job."[4] Still, Ginsburg seemed as surprised as everyone else in 1995 when Rehnquist added four gold stripes to each sleeve of his black robe, inspired by the Lord Chancellor's costume in a local production of Gilbert and Sullivan's *Iolanthe.* "Why did a man not given to sartorial splendor decide on such a costume?" Ginsburg asked. "In his own words, he did not wish to be upstaged by the women. (Justice O'Connor has several attractive neck pieces, collars from British gowns, and a frilly French foulard; I wear British and French lace foulards, too, and sometimes one of French Canadian design.)"

What Ginsburg appreciated most about Rehnquist was his willingness to change his mind in cases involving gender discrimination. When she joined the Court, he was one of three justices who had sat on the bench during her arguments in the 1970s, and he had voted against her in many of her landmark cases. He was the only dissenter in the eight-to-one *Frontiero* decision, where Ginsburg persuaded the Court in 1973 that the military cannot distribute benefits to the families of service members on the basis of sex, and in the eight-to-one decision in *Taylor v. Louisiana* (1975), where she persuaded the Court that the exclusion of women from jury panels violates the Sixth Amendment right to an impartial jury trial. And because of his devotion to federalism, Rehnquist, along with his Stanford Law School classmate O'Connor, continued to vote against Ginsburg in important cases involving gender discrimination on the Supreme Court, including *United States v.*

Morrison in 2000, when Rehnquist wrote the five-to-four majority opinion striking down part of the federal Violence Against Women Act. Still, Ginsburg was especially heartened when Rehnquist, in the 2003 case *Nevada Department of Human Resources v. Hibbs,* upheld the right of state employees to recover damages for violations of the federal Family and Medical Leave Act. She also never forgot that Rehnquist voted with her in one of the cases that meant the most to her, the Virginia Military Institute case.

Justice Ginsburg was distraught by Rehnquist's death from thyroid cancer in 2005. And when John Roberts succeeded him later that year, she was well disposed to the new chief, as he was to her. She had admired his skills as a Supreme Court advocate; he had appeared frequently before the Court in the 1990s. And as he took office, Chief Justice Roberts was impressed by Ginsburg's reputation for judicial minimalism, which he thought would help him in his quest to persuade his colleagues to converge around narrow, unanimous opinions that avoided divisive constitutional questions. As it turned out, however, the Roberts Court produced a series of hotly contested five-to-four decisions that Ginsburg thought were deeply misguided, with majority opinions written by the chief or by Justice Kennedy and the principal dissent written by Justice Ginsburg herself. They included the 2010 case *Citizens United v. Federal Election Commission,* which Roberts had initially wanted to decide more narrowly, and the 2013 voting rights case *Shelby County v. Holder,* which Ginsburg considered an act of "hubris." She also lamented Roberts's decision to join his fellow conservatives in *National Federation of Independent Business v. Sebelius* in 2012, in which they held that Congress had no power, under the Commerce Clause, to pass the Affordable Care Act. (Roberts's decision to switch his vote and to uphold the ACA as a tax did not entirely mollify Ginsburg's concerns.) Still, Ginsburg, like Roberts, is devoted to preserving the nonpartisan legitimacy of the Supreme Court, and like the chief justice she has long denounced attacks on judicial independence by partisan politicians.

JR: You were an admirer of Chief Justice Rehnquist. How have the workings of the Court changed under Chief Justice Roberts?

RBG: I was very fond of the old chief. I am also an admirer of the current chief, who has extraordinary skills as an advocate. He was a repeat player at oral argument, always super prepared, engaging in his presentation, and nimble in responding to the Court's questions. As to the change, I regard the Roberts/Rehnquist change as a "like-kind exchange," an expression tax lawyers use. Our current chief is a bit more flexible at oral argument: he won't stop a lawyer or a justice in mid-sentence when the red light goes on. And at our conference, he's a little more relaxed about allowing time for cross-table discussion. As to his decisions, there's not a major shift. I'm hoping that as our current chief gets older, he may end up the way Rehnquist did when he wrote for the Court upholding the Family and Medical Leave Act in 2003. That's a decision you wouldn't have believed he would ever write when he joined the Court in the early seventies. Chief Justice Rehnquist also decided that, as much as he disliked the *Miranda* decision, it had become police culture, and he wasn't going to overrule it.

JR: There have still been some big five-to-four decisions during Chief Justice Roberts's tenure, including *Hobby Lobby,* where you criticized your male colleagues for having a "blind spot" on women's issues. Given the chief justice's preference for unanimity, how have your dissents in those cases been received within the Court?

RBG: My answer to that would be, at least as well as Scalia's attention-grabbing dissents.

JR: This idea of consensus is much discussed, and Chief Justice Roberts came to office saying that he wanted there to be more consensus, fewer five-to-four decisions, but he's had mixed success. This term was a bit better. It was only 15 percent of the cases that were five-to-four. But there's some very strong rhetoric that's going on out there. Will Chief Justice Roberts achieve consensus, and is consensus a good thing?

RBG: I don't think he meant by that that he or any one of us would surrender a deeply held view. You know, the Court is not like a legislature; we don't vote a particular way because we would like that outcome. We have to account for everything we do by giving reasons for it. So there's no cross-trading at all on the Court. What there can be is, instead of deciding the great big issue, we can agree on a lower ground, on a procedural issue, perhaps. Justice Sandra Day O'Connor was a grand master at that — getting the Court to come together on a ground on which we could agree, and defer the bigger battle for another day.

JR: She was a master, and you also are famous for your incremental, narrow, and restrained decisions. And yet many of the decisions in recent terms have not been narrow. The *Citizens United* case could have been decided on very narrow grounds, but instead it was quite broad. Do you think the chief justice is really committed to narrow opinions?

RBG: I can't answer that question. The majority saw *Citizens United* as presenting a very basic First Amendment issue, one that needed to be decided sooner rather than later. You're quite right that it could have been decided on a lesser ground. We started out the term with that five-to-four decision, and if you read our opinions, I think you will find that both sides are very well stated.

I should explain how things work at the Court. When the Court is sitting, we sit two weeks in a row; we meet on Wednesday afternoon to talk about Monday's cases, and on Friday morning to talk about Tuesday's and Wednesday's cases. The chief starts by summarizing a case and then expressing his tentative vote. When all of us have had our say, the chief justice will give us our homework. That is, he will assign people to write the opinions from the sitting. When he's not in the majority, the most senior justice in the majority has that job. Maybe twice a term, the opinion will come out not as the conference voted initially, but on the other side. To give you an illustration of how it really ain't over until it's over, I remember a case where the conference vote was seven-to-two. I was one of the two, and I was assigned to write the dissent. In the fullness of time, the decision became six-to-three, but my two became six. So we are constantly trying to persuade each other. We do it mainly through our writing, and it will happen that a justice who was on one side will read the dissenting opinion and say, "I think the dissent has it right; I'm going to join that side."

JR: Let's talk about Chief Justice Rehnquist, who came around in the gender cases. How did you persuade him, or how was he persuaded?

RBG: As long as one lives, one can learn.

And the best example of that is his decision for the Court in the case upholding the Family and Medical Leave Act. The chief had two daughters, he had two granddaughters. Maybe more granddaughters, but two from his oldest child. And I think he was devoted to the girls. When his daughter Janet divorced, I think he felt that the girls, her girls, needed a male presence in their lives. And nobody saw this . . . nobody who came to the Court and saw the chief would ever appreciate how devoted he was to those two girls, and how much they loved him.

JR: Now, if I were channeling the Justice Scalia character in the opera, I would say, this is completely inappropriate — "The Constitution says absolutely nothing about this!" The law is supposed to be faithful to the original understanding; it shouldn't evolve, it shouldn't change. Why should the chief justice take into account his daughter's views or his granddaughters' prospects? Is that an appropriate thing for a justice to do?

RBG: They are representative of the change in society, the change in parents' aspirations for their daughters or their support of their daughters' aspirations.

JR: This is such a hard question to teach, and everyone wants to know the answer: How does the Court take into account changes in society?

RBG: Well, in this case, in the Family and Medical Leave Act, it was easy, because it was a law passed by Congress, and Congress's authority was challenged as outside the domain of the federal government. So the chief explained why this law was national business, was a matter that the national government had the authority to deal with.

JR: Justice Rehnquist voted against you when you were an advocate in the 1970s, but you always kept your cool.

RBG: Yes, because I wanted to win my case. I came to love my old chief, especially after he wrote the decision upholding the Family and Medical Leave Act, but my very last argument in the Supreme Court was in the fall of 1978. It was a case about putting women on juries. Young people today are astonished when they are told it was not all that long ago when women were either not put on the jury roll — they could opt in if they wanted to, but they were not called otherwise — or they were on the roll, but a woman, any woman, was exempt.

So I divided that argument with the public defender from Kansas City, Missouri. I had fifteen minutes, and I was about to sit down, confident that I had gotten out everything I wanted to convey. And then Justice Rehnquist commented, "So, Mrs. Ginsburg, you won't settle for Susan B. Anthony's face on the new dollar." Chief Justice Burger said something polite, and that was that, argument over. In the cab going back to Union Station, I thought, "Ugh, why wasn't I quick enough to think of a perfect comeback, which would have been no, Your Honor, tokens won't do."

It was not so long ago that most of the social clubs in New York and Washington, DC, were men only. So whenever I was asked to speak at those clubs, I said, "I'm not going to speak at a place that wouldn't welcome me as a member." Some very distinguished groups. The American Law Institute, for example, when they met in New York, they dined at the Century Association. I wrote out an explanation of why they should not be meeting there. Most people agreed with me. Some people didn't, especially when the ALI switched to the Harvard Club, where the food was not comparable.

My first encounter with men-only social clubs happened when my husband was working for a law firm in New York. The firm had a holiday party at a club that did not admit women. The women associates let it be known that that was improper. They weren't listened to. So the next year, none of the women associates showed up at the holiday party. The year after that, the holiday party was held at a place that welcomed women as well as men.

JR: It's extraordinary to think of how different things were — a world where women couldn't go to holiday parties or join clubs. Does it seem like extraordinary progress, or is it inadequate? What is your assessment of the progress we have made since then?

RBG: The progress has been enormous, and that is what makes me hopeful for the future. The signs are all around us. I think there will be more women running for office than ever before at every level — local, state, federal. When I was nominated for the good job I now have, the Senate was conscious that there were no women on the Judiciary Committee, so they added two for my nomination, and they have never gone back to an all-male committee since then.

8
WHEN A DISSENT
SPARKED A MEME

Justice Ginsburg has long marveled at her transformation into a judicial celebrity. In a 1996 speech, she compared the change in her life to what Virginia Woolf describes in her novel *Orlando,* whose central character lives for centuries as a man and awakens one morning as a woman. "Looking at herself in the mirror, Orlando is not displeased," Ginsburg said. " 'Same person,' she says, 'just another sex!' But her life becomes distinctly different, the world treats her differently because she's a woman, although in mind and spirit she's the same person." Ginsburg reported that, in her case, a private life had become a public one. "Now trivial things are noticed. In the same month, soon after the U.S. Senate confirmed my nomination to the Court, I made the Style page of the *New York Times* and the *People* magazine list of America's Worst Dressed," she said. "When the press reported that I read mail by flashlight during cinema previews, I received a half-dozen pocket lights from caring people across the country."[1]

Still, this media attention in the 1990s was mild compared to the dramatic transformation in Ginsburg's celebrity when she became, in the summer of 2013, an internet sensation and then an American icon. That July, Shana Knizhnik, a New York University law student, created the Tumblr blog *Notorious R.B.G.* Knizhnik had been inspired by Ginsburg's dissenting opinion the previous month in *Shelby County v. Holder,* which she quoted on her newly created blog. "Throwing out preclearance when it has worked and is continuing to work to stop discriminatory changes is like throwing away your umbrella in a rainstorm because you are not getting wet,"[2] Ginsburg had written, objecting to the Court's five-to-four decision to strike down Section 5 of the Voting Rights Act, which required states with a history of voting discrimination to get the federal government's approval, or "preclearance," before any changes to their voting rules could go into effect. Invoking the rapper Notorious B.I.G., Knizhnik said she had been moved to create the Tumblr blog because "Ginsburg defies stereotypes. People expect this meek, grandmotherly type. She is a grandmother, but she shows so much strength, and she is who she is without apology."[3] The Tumblr blog went viral, and Knizhnik went on to write a book, *Notorious RBG: The Life and Times of Ruth Bader Ginsburg,* with the journalist Irin Carmon, who explained that Ginsburg "allows women to imagine a different kind of power and to visualize a woman in power well past an age where she is usually invisible to society."[4]

As Ginsburg's celebrity grew, her dissenting opinions became increasingly fiery. "The Court, I fear, has ventured into a minefield," she wrote in her dissent from the five-to-four *Hobby Lobby* decision that allowed employers to exempt themselves from regulations that conflicted with their religious beliefs. "Would the exemption . . . extend to employers with religiously grounded objections to blood transfusions (Jehovah's Witnesses); antidepressants (Scientologists); medications derived from pigs, including anesthesia, intravenous fluids, and pills coated with gelatin (certain Muslims, Jews, and Hindus); and vaccinations?"[5]

When I interviewed Justice Ginsburg in September 2014, a year after her Tumblr apotheosis, I asked about the topic that

169

most surprised me as a friend and a journalist: How had the restrained judicial minimalist, the judge's judge, whose speeches from the 1990s emphasized the importance of civility and collegiality, been transformed into the fiery leader of the opposition? She insisted that she hadn't changed, but that the Court had changed with Justice O'Connor's retirement in 2006. As she found herself more frequently in dissent, she felt an obligation to express her disagreement clearly. It was in the spring of 2007 that Ginsburg first issued two widely noted dissenting opinions — in *Gonzales v. Carhart,* the five-to-four decision upholding the federal partial-birth abortion ban, and in *Ledbetter v. Goodyear Tire and Rubber Company,* the five-to-four decision holding that a woman had waited too long to file a federal pay discrimination claim. For many, those two cases marked the beginning of the emergence of the great dissenter who became Notorious RBG. But Ginsburg also signaled that another turning point was the retirement of Justice John Paul Stevens in 2010.

To understand how Ginsburg's role changed, it may be helpful to review the way Supreme Court majority opinions and dissents get assigned. As Ginsburg noted in the previous chapter, the justices meet in a private conference twice a week when the Court is in session to vote on which cases to decide and how to decide the cases that have just been argued. No one except the nine justices is allowed in the conference room. In order of seniority, each justice discusses the case, with the chief justice speaking first and the most junior justice speaking last, and then the justices vote. If the chief justice is in the majority — that is, if at least four other justices agree with his position — he can write the majority opinion himself or assign it to another justice. If the chief justice is in the minority, then the senior associate justice in the majority serves as a shadow chief — she can write the majority decision herself or assign it to the justice who best reflects the majority's views. When Justice Ginsburg succeeded Stevens as the most senior liberal associate justice, she told me, she tried to persuade her liberal colleagues to speak in one voice when they were in dissent, so that their views would carry more force in persuading the public. That's why, in these cases, there is often a principal dissenting opinion, written by Ginsburg and joined by all three of the other liberal justices.

Still, this change in role doesn't entirely

account for Ginsburg's transformation. In several high-profile cases, the more pragmatic liberal justices (Elena Kagan and Stephen Breyer) have been willing to reach across the aisle to form centrist compromise positions with Chief Justice John Roberts. In the Affordable Care Act case, *National Federation of Independent Business v. Sebelius,* for example, Kagan and Breyer joined the conservative justices in holding that the Medicaid expansion was unconstitutional, but they agreed with Roberts that the expansion could take effect if the states viewed it as optional rather than mandatory. By contrast, Justices Ginsburg and Sotomayor insisted that a mandatory Medicaid expansion would be consistent with the Constitution. Ginsburg joined Justice Sotomayor's dissenting opinion from the Court's seven-to-two decision in *Trump v. Hawaii* (2018), upholding President Trump's travel ban, where Kagan and Breyer agreed with the conservative justices. And Sotomayor joined Ginsburg's dissent in *Masterpiece Cakeshop v. Colorado Civil Rights Commission,* where the other seven justices ruled narrowly in favor of a baker who refused on First Amendment grounds to bake a wedding cake for a gay couple.

Because Ginsburg, like Sotomayor, is less

willing to join the more moderate liberal justices in searching for centrist compromises and more willing to file separate dissents, it seems fair to conclude that she has evolved from the days before her appointment to the Supreme Court, when she expressed concern about dissents and emphasized the importance of judicial unanimity and collegiality. In a series of articles before her nomination, she said that too frequent use of separate opinions by appellate courts would threaten their authority.[6] In a 1990 article, "Remarks on Writing Separately," she had worried that the U.S. Supreme Court was filing too many separate opinions, which she said could undermine the clarity and stability of its decisions.[7] In her Madison Lecture at New York University, in 1992, she suggested that when appellate "panels are unanimous, the standard practice, to encourage brevity and speed, should be to issue the decision per curiam" — that is, in the name of the Court — "without disclosing the opinion writer."[8] And she endorsed Justice Louis Brandeis's view that in cases with what she called "grand constitutional questions . . . it is best that the matter be definitively settled, preferably with one opinion." In other articles before her appointment, she had emphasized the importance of moderation and collegiality as the ideal qualities for judges and stressed the importance of maintaining impartiality by crossing party lines.[9]

In Ginsburg's view, she has been moved to file strong dissents in five-to-four cases because an increasingly conservative Supreme Court has refused to engage in the kind of collegiality and compromise she views as essential. And as Ginsburg the minimalist evolved into the Notorious RBG, she has not indulged in what she called, quoting the legal scholar Roscoe Pound, the "intemperate denunciation of [the writers'] colleagues, violent invective, attributi[on] of bad motives to the majority of the court, and insinuations of incompetence, negligence, prejudice, or obtuseness of [other judges]"[10] that she identified in 1992 as threatening public respect for the courts.

Ginsburg is now convinced, however, of the value of dissenting opinions in persuading future generations to correct perceived injustice. "Dissents speak to a future age," she told the NPR journalist Nina Totenberg in 2002. "The greatest dissents do become court opinions and gradually over time their views become the dominant view. So that's the dissenter's hope: that they are writing not for today but for tomorrow."[11] This view was fortified in her 2007 dissent in *Ledbetter v. Goodyear Tire and Rubber Co.,* where she denounced a five-to-four conservative majority for holding that Lilly Ledbetter, a Goodyear employee, hadn't filed her sex discrimination claims within the time period mandated by Congress. Ginsburg's dissent criticized the majority's "cramped" interpretation for ignoring the broad goals of federal antidiscrimination laws and called on Congress to overturn the decision. And in January 2009, Congress responded to Ginsburg's invitation by passing the Lilly Ledbetter Fair Pay Act, which President Barack Obama signed on his first day in office.

JR: You are famously a huge opera fan. But recently you've become an internet sensation because of another kind of music. There are all these T-shirts going around the internet saying NOTORIOUS R.B.G. So my first question is: Do you even know who the Notorious B.I.G. is?

RBG: My law clerks told me. It's not the first T-shirt. The first one appeared after *Bush v. Gore.* Those T-shirts showed my picture and, under it, the words I DISSENT.

175

Now there are many take-offs on the NOTO-RIOUS R.B.G. shirt. Another T-shirt, done after the *Shelby County* decision, displays I LOVE R.B.G.

JR: There's also a WHAT WOULD RUTH BADER GINSBURG DO?

RBG: And another: YOU CAN'T SPELL TRUTH WITHOUT RUTH.

JR: How do you feel about having become an internet sensation?

RBG: My grandchildren love it. At my advanced age — I'm now an octogenarian — I'm constantly amazed by the number of people who want to take my picture.

JR: When you were appointed, many people called you a minimalist. They said you were cautious. It's only in recent years that you really found your voice and have become this liberal icon. What changed?

RBG: Jeff, I don't think I changed. Perhaps I am a little less tentative than I was when I was a new justice. But what really changed was the composition of the Court. Think of 2006, when Justice O'Connor left us, and in the months after she was replaced, in the cases in which the Court divided five to four and I was one of the four, but I would have been one among the five if Justice O'Connor had remained. So I don't think that my jurisprudence has changed, but the issues coming before the Court are getting a different reception.

JR: But it seems that in the past few years, really, you're on fire. You're sounding like Louis Brandeis, using words like *hubris* as a fit word for the demolition of the Voting Rights Act in *Shelby County.* You have these wonderful metaphors about umbrellas and getting wet. And my question is: What emboldened you or freed you up to express yourself so powerfully recently in a way that you hadn't before?

RBG: I had a good model. For most of my years on the Court, Justice John Paul Stevens was the most senior justice. When we split five to four, he was the most senior among the four. He was fair in his distribution of dissents, but he did keep most of the major cases for himself.

I try to be fair, so no one ends up with all the dull cases while another has all the exciting cases. I do take, I suppose, more than a fair share of the dissenting opinions in the most-watched cases.

JR: So it's really a question of your role. And as you say, as the senior associate justice, you have the prerogative, when you're in the majority, to either write the decision yourself or assign it to the judge you think will do the best job. And when you're in dissent, you can write the principal dissent yourself or assign it to whom you like. How are you using this power? Have you put a premium on unanimity, and are you trying to convince the four dissenters, when they're together, to all join the same opinion?

RBG: Yes. I met with my colleagues in the Affordable Care Act case. I think we spent almost three hours just talking about how the dissent should be written. I asked for any suggestions my colleagues had. They saw the draft of my opinion before it circulated to the full Court, so I could make sure I am speaking for the four of us, and not just for myself. I think it's much easier for the public to comprehend one dissent instead of four. So we make a deliberate effort not to splinter. Sometimes, not often, it's unavoidable. But for the most part, we can come together in a dissent that speaks for all the dissenters.

JR: This vision that you're setting out, of the four liberals being united against the five conservatives, is very different from the one Chief Justice Roberts offered when he took office, when he talked about the importance of unanimity and trying to persuade his colleagues to converge around narrow, unanimous opinions to avoid these five-to-four splits, because it's bad for the Court and bad for the country to make the Court look political. Is that a tenable vision? Has he had any success? Is it realistic, or is the Court just going to continue to issue the most important decisions by five-to-four polarized votes?

RBG: What he projected as desirable — in his very first term, the Court was unusually together. And there's a clear explanation for that: the first term of Chief Justice Roberts was also the last term of Justice Sandra Day O'Connor. So, her last year, his first year, there was more unanimity than we have seen since. I've said a number of times, and I think anyone who checked would find it's true, that the year she left us, in every case where I was among the four, if she had remained, I would have been among the five. So her leaving the Court made an enormous difference.

JR: And you've discouraged separate concurrences.

RBG: Yes.

JR: Why is that?

RBG: The experience I don't want to see repeated occurred in *Bush v. Gore.* The Court divided five to four. There were four separate dissents, and that confused the press. In fact, some of the reporters announced that the decision was seven-to-two. If we had time, the four of us would have gotten together, and there might have been one dissent instead of filling far too many pages in the *U.S. Reports* with our separate dissents.

JR: Generally, you've been more reluctant to compromise than some of your colleagues. Is that a conscious decision?

RBG: That was so in *Bush v. Gore.* It was also true more recently in the *Hobby Lobby* case, where Justices Breyer and Kagan said we'd rather not take a position on a for-profit corporation's free-exercise rights.

JR: So they wrote a separate dissent.

RBG: Just a few lines of explanation. We all agreed on what was most important. It didn't matter whether the business was a sole proprietorship, a partnership, a corporation. The simple point is, we have the right to speak freely, to exercise religion freely, with this key limit. As Professor Chafee explained, "We have the right to swing our arm until it hits the other fellow's nose." [Zechariah Chafee Jr. taught at Harvard Law School from 1916 to 1956.] I should emphasize that none of us questioned the genuineness of the *Hobby Lobby* owners' belief. That was a given. But no one who is in business for profit can foist his or her beliefs on a workforce that includes many people who do not share those beliefs.

JR: When you tell that story of the expansion of equality coming from constitutional amendments and from the civil rights movement and from acts of Congress, I think I begin to understand the passion of your dissents in cases like voting rights and affirmative action and health care. Let's talk about the voting rights dissent, where the rhetoric was unforgettable. You say, "Early attempts to cope with this vile infection resembled battling the Hydra. Whenever one form of voting discrimination was identified and prohibited, others sprang up in its place." Were you surprised that Texas decided to implement a voter ID law just hours after the Court struck down Section 5 of the Voting Rights Act in *Shelby County v. Holder*?

RBG: No. Well, that was the metaphor about putting down the umbrella because we weren't getting wet, but the storm is raging. I expected exactly that to happen. Now it's a problem what to do — the voter ID laws, closing the polls early, putting polling places in inconvenient places.

JR: Are Sections 2 and 3 of the Voting Rights Act, which remain, adequate alternatives, or might the Court cut back on those as well?

RBG: I can't predict what the courts will do, but perhaps we should explain. Section 3 is the "bail-in" provision. It was one of the reasons I thought the Voting Rights Act was constitutional. Suppose a state that was, in 1965, one of those states that did not allow African Americans to vote, but over the years, they had changed their ways and they were no longer keeping people away from the polls because of their race. If they have a clean record for ten years, they can bail out of the law's requirements. And on the other hand, if a state that was not in the group required to preclear voting changes originally, those states or districts could be bailed in, if warranted. So there was a way to take out political units that didn't belong there and add ones that did. That was the mechanism that Congress provided. But I don't think there was anything said in the majority opinion about the bail-in, bail-out provisions.

JR: Courts, though, have imposed a very high requirement of intentional discrimination before allowing states to be bailed in, which is why very few have been bailed in, and these suits may not succeed for that reason.

RBG: Yes. That remained to be seen.

JR: And Section 2 also requires a high degree of intentional discrimination, and even though Congress tried to lower the standard, the Court has cut that back as well, so it's a similarly uphill battle.

RBG: Well, the Congress said it's discriminatory in effect, even if you can't prove intent. What the Court will do with that is an open question.

JR: But so much of the power of your dissent came from the need, as you said, for Section 5. Congress legitimately concluded that preclearance by the federal government was necessary, because unless you could challenge this second generation of voting discrimination in advance, the Hydra, as you put it, would return. Tell us more about that.

RBG: Yes, in different forms, the original devices were blatant. There was no disguising what they were doing. The literacy tests in the old days — well, just the intimidation of black voters, even if they were able to get to the poll to register, there were people stopping them from doing that. I mean, it was a violent history that accounts for the Voting Rights Act. And then, over time, those devices, those crude devices, passed, but more subtle devices emerged, like putting a polling place in an area that's inconvenient for minority voters to reach, or opening the polls late and closing them early, making it difficult for people who have jobs to come out to vote, also redistricting. More subtle, more sophisticated devices have replaced the old, crude devices. And that, we can see, is happening right now.

JR: And you made a very strong argument that the framers of the Fourteenth and Fifteenth Amendments intended Congress, not the courts, to be the primary defender of voting rights.

RBG: Yes. If you compare — take the First Amendment; it says, "Congress shall make no law." It says, "Congress keep your hands off." But the Thirteenth, Fourteenth, and Fifteenth Amendments end in "Congress shall have the power to enforce" those post–Civil War amendments by appropriate legislation. So the Constitution, instead of being a negative check on what the legislature can do, is affirmatively giving the legislature the authority to implement those amendments.

JR: You were also critical of the Court's expansion in *Shelby County* of the opinion in *Northwest Austin Municipal Utility District No. 1 v. Holder,* which, a few years earlier, had avoided the constitutional decision on the Voting Rights Act. That was an example of Chief Justice Roberts avoiding a constitutional conflict by ruling narrowly, but are you sorry, in retrospect, that you joined *Northwest Austin?*

RBG: I think the result in *Northwest Austin* was right. This was a water district that had never discriminated, but was in a state that had. The Court read the act to say: districts, municipalities, counties could bail out. So you could be part of a state where discrimination was still going on, but in your area, there was no discrimination. *Northwest Austin* established that bail-out was available to smaller political units, a good thing. The chief wrote the opinion, and he put in language that came back to haunt some of us.

JR: What did you mean when you said the Roberts Court is turning into one of the most activist in history?

RBG: I should define the term *activism* as I used it for that purpose. It is a court that is not at all hesitant to overturn legislation passed by the Congress. So to take two very recent headline examples. The Affordable

Care Act passed Congress, but the Court — well, the Court held that the Commerce Clause didn't go that far. Thank goodness there was the taxing power, which saved the case. But the readiness to strike down a piece of legislation under the Commerce Clause — insurance is surely commerce — it was just astounding to me.

The worst case, I think, was *Shelby County.* The amendments to the Voting Rights Act passed Congress overwhelmingly. I think it was unanimous in the Senate, and three hundred and thirty-some-odd votes in the House. If anyone knows about the Voting Rights Act — how it affects the system — I think the elected representatives have an appreciation that unelected judges don't have. And yet, despite the overwhelming majority in Congress that passed the Voting Rights Act, the Court said: it won't do. The formula is out of date, so Congress would have to go back and take this up. The Voting Rights Act passed originally in 1965 during Johnson's tenure. It was renewed during the tenure of Nixon, Ford, both Bushes. But the Court said: it won't do. So that's an example of striking down legislation on a subject that the people in the political arena are better informed about than the Court is.

JR: I want to close by asking you this: Do you expect your dissents to become majority opinions in the future or, on the contrary, do you think that affirmative action will fall, that campaign finance will be further restricted, that *Roe* will be overturned? Do you think in the future you will be in the majority or continue to be in dissent?

RBG: Sometimes Congress is helpful. There's a difference between a case that involves constitutional interpretation, where the Court says, "This is what the Constitution means." Well, that's what it means until the Court overrules its decision or there's a constitutional amendment. But when you're dealing with statutes like our principal employment discrimination law, Title VII, if the Court gets it wrong, Congress can fix it.

And so, one of my most satisfying times on the Court was the Lilly Ledbetter case, when my dissent said, essentially, "Congress, my colleagues really misunderstood what you meant, so make it even clearer," which Congress did inside of two years. The case concerned a woman who was an area manager at a Goodyear tire plant. It was a job that had been held dominantly by men. And Lilly Ledbetter, after she worked there for well over a decade, someone put a slip of paper in her mailbox and it just had numbers on it. It was Lilly's salary and the pay of all the men doing the same job. The most junior man was making more than Lilly. So she brought a Title VII suit and said, "Looks like discrimination to me." The jury agreed; she got a substantial verdict. Came to our Court, and we said she sued too late. Title VII says you have to complain within one hundred eighty days of the discriminatory event. This pay discrimination started in the seventies. Well, think of a woman in Lilly Ledbetter's situation. First, the employer doesn't give out pay information, so how would she know? Second, if she suspected she wasn't treated as well as her male counterparts, she would also be concerned, "If I complain and if I bring a suit, the defense will probably be: 'It has nothing to do with Lilly's being a woman; she just doesn't do the job as well.'" Then, if she goes on, and she's there for ten years, and she's getting good performance ratings, that defense is no longer available; they can't say she doesn't do the job well. So she has a winnable case at that point. She can show the pay disparity, she can show that she did the job as well, or better, than the men. But the Court says, "Now that you have a winnable case, it's too late."

So my dissent described what every woman of Lilly's generation knew: that if you are the first woman in a field that has been occupied by men, you don't want to be known as a complainer; you don't want to rock the boat; you don't want to be seen as a troublemaker. But there comes a point when the discrimination is staring you in the face, and you have to make a stand. And that's what Lilly did. The idea that the dissent put forward was the soul of simplicity. It said, "Every paycheck that this woman receives is renewing the discrimination, so she can sue within one hundred eighty days of her latest paycheck, and she will be on time." That's what Congress said: "Yes, that's what we meant."

As I said, the Constitution is something else, and the Court has, time and again, seen that it has made mistakes and has corrected them.

If it's a constitutional case, Congress can't fix it. The change would have to come about either through constitutional amendment — and our Constitution is powerfully hard to amend: it takes two-thirds of Congress and three-quarters of the states to ratify. I know from experience with the Equal Rights Amendment how hard it is to amend the Constitution, so the next best thing is for —

not the next best thing, it is the better thing — is for the Court to correct the mistake it has made. We've had a long tradition of dissents becoming the law of the land. One example, the free speech dissents of Justices Holmes and Brandeis. Another example is the dreadful *Dred Scott* decision. There were two dissenters who recognized the Court was wrong. Then there was the first Justice John Marshall Harlan, who dissented in the so-called Civil Rights Cases, and then, some thirteen years later, in *Plessy v. Ferguson.* I think it's good when we look back to see that there were people who thought the Court's judgment was wrong and wrote the judgment that was right — it starts out as a dissent and then, in the next generations, becomes the opinion of the Court.

9
THE CASES SHE
WOULD OVERTURN

Ever since she was an appellate judge, Ruth Bader Ginsburg has viewed herself as an apostle of judicial minimalism, meaning that judges should decide cases narrowly rather than broadly. She has also said repeatedly that justices should generally defer to other decision makers (Congress, state legislatures, state courts) and should be guided by "measured motion," meaning that they should not leap too far ahead of public opinion and should, in most cases, respect judicial precedents rather than eviscerating them.

In a revealing conversation, she provided me with an explanation of the rare circumstances in which she thinks judicial invalidation of laws is warranted, and she identified the Supreme Court cases she is most eager to see overturned.

She explained that her lone dissent from the Court's 2013 decision in *Fisher v.*

University of Texas, which overturned a lower court ruling that had upheld the university's affirmative action program and sent the case back to the lower court with orders to apply "strict judicial scrutiny," had been inspired by the most famous footnote in Supreme Court history.

That footnote, well known to law students as "footnote 4," appears in a 1938 case called *United States v. Carolene Products.* The opinion of the Court was written by Chief Justice Harlan Fiske Stone, and it held that courts generally should uphold economic regulations because it is not the role of judges to second-guess legislative decisions, except in cases when those decisions themselves might be infected by racial prejudice or other flaws in the political process.

Decided right after the Supreme Court got out of the business of second-guessing the economic legislation of Franklin Roosevelt's New Deal, *Carolene Products* was the Supreme Court's most systematic attempt in the twentieth century to identify the circumstances in which judges should strike down laws. When considering economic legislation, Stone said, judges should presume the laws are constitutional. But in footnote 4, he identified three circumstances where "the presumption of constitutionality" might not apply and where laws should be "subjected to more exacting judicial scrutiny": first, in cases where the law violated a specific prohibition written down in the text of the Constitution or the Bill of Rights; second, in cases where laws restrict the "political processes which can ordinarily be expected to bring about repeal of undesirable legislation," such as laws restricting freedom of speech; and third, laws "directed at particular religious, or national, or racial minorities or other laws infected by prejudice against discrete and insular minorities."

Ginsburg studied footnote 4 at Harvard Law School, and following the convention of many scholars and judges, she compressed Stone's three categories into two, which she said had defined the Supreme Court's outlook in constitutional cases for most of the twentieth century. The Court generally upheld economic legislation, Ginsburg noted, and was more skeptical of laws that disadvantaged religious, national, or racial minorities, or other groups disadvantaged in the political process by prejudicial stereotypes, such as African Americans.

Ginsburg told me that, in the *Fisher* case, she disagreed with her colleagues that affirmative action laws should be subject to searching judicial scrutiny, arguing that these laws were designed to help minorities rather than hurt them.

Ginsburg's invocation of footnote 4 is significant because it provides a comprehensive theory for identifying the cases she would most like to see overturned — namely, cases in which a conservative majority struck down laws that neither violated a clear prohibition in the Constitution nor were examples of majorities disadvantaging minorities. That list includes cases where Ginsburg believes that the conservatives were engaging in the kind of economic judicial activism that the Supreme Court repudiated in the *Carolene Products* case in the 1930s, such as the *Citizens United* case, holding that corporations had the same free speech rights as natural persons, and the part of the Affordable Care Act decision holding that Congress had no power, under its authority to regulate interstate commerce, to mandate the purchase of health insurance.

Ginsburg's list also includes cases where the conservative justices struck down laws designed to help minorities, such as parts of the Voting Rights Act and affirmative action programs. And footnote 4 provides an explanation of cases where Ginsburg thinks that judicial intervention was justified, but where the conservative justices voted instead for restraint. Her examples include *Gonzales v. Carhart* (2007), where the conservative justices voted to uphold the federal ban on partial-birth abortion, which Ginsburg felt disadvantaged women, and *United States v. Windsor* and *Hollingsworth v. Perry* (both 2013), where Justice Kennedy joined the liberals in voting to strike down the federal Defense of Marriage Act, or DOMA, on the grounds that it disadvantaged gays and lesbians. Ginsburg also singles out two earlier decisions, *Maher v. Roe* (1977) and *Harris v. McRae* (1980), which held that Congress and the states did not have to extend Medicaid coverage for abortions to poor women, whether or not the abortions were medically necessary.

For Ginsburg, as for the justices of the Warren and Burger Courts of the 1950s, '60s, and '70s, judges should generally uphold laws passed by majorities that favor minorities, unless there is strong evidence that the political process is not working. That simple theory, which she learned at Harvard Law School, once defined the Supreme Court's approach in constitutional cases; Justice Ginsburg hopes it will be resurrected in the future.

■ ■ ■ ■

JR: What's the worst ruling the current Court has produced?

RBG: If there was one decision I would overrule, it would be *Citizens United.* I think the notion that we have all the democracy that money can buy strays so far from what our democracy is supposed to be. So that's number one on my list. Number two would be the part of the health care decision [*National Federation of Independent Business v. Sebelius*] that concerns the Commerce Clause. Since 1937, the Court has allowed Congress a very free hand in enacting social and economic legislation. I thought that the attempt of the Court to intrude on Congress's domain in that area had stopped by the end of the 1930s. Of course, health care involves commerce.

Perhaps number three would be *Shelby County,* involving essentially the destruction of the Voting Rights Act. That act had a voluminous legislative history. The bill extending the Voting Rights Act was passed overwhelmingly by both houses, Republicans and Democrats; everyone was on board. The Court's interference with that decision of the political branches seemed to me out of order. The Court should have respected the legislative judgment. Legislators know much more about elections than the Court does. And the same was true of *Citizens United.* I think members of the legislature, people who have to run for office, know the connection between money and influence on what laws get passed. The majority's position was, that was 1965; it's many years later; some states that discriminated may not be discriminating anymore. So Congress has to come up with a new formula. Well, what member of Congress is going to stand up and say, "My district is still discriminating"? I thought my colleagues were not as restrained as they should be because they should have respected the overwhelming vote in the Congress to renew the Voting Rights Act.

And fourth is *Gonzales v. Carhart,* the so-called partial-birth abortion case. This is a medical procedure that is no one's first choice, but it may be the only option for a woman, and the Court refused to recognize that a ban on such a procedure overlooked that some women had no other choice, so that's a decision I would like to see overruled. If you go back in time — in two decisions from the seventies, the Supreme Court held that Medicaid coverage was not available for any abortion, therapeutic or non-therapeutic. Which left us with the situation in our country where any woman of means, any woman who can afford to go to another state, will have access to abortion. The people who won't are poor people who can't travel, who can't take off days from work. And that's a sorry situation. I think it is most unfortunate that the people who are disadvantaged are the most voiceless people, poor women. So that decision and other restrictive abortion decisions I would like to see overruled.

JR: And why did you decide to dissent alone in *Fisher,* the affirmative action case? Here, once again, the majority was avoiding ruling squarely on the constitutional question, but the fear was that the standard was actually being raised in a way that might lead down the road to the end of affirmative action.

RBG: I thought that the Court was taking an astonishing position, if you go back to the origin of the suspect classification doctrine. It came out of a footnote in a decision by Chief Justice Stone in the *Carolene Products* case, where he explained that, for the most part, we trust the legislative process, and the Court is deferential, respectful, of the laws that Congress passes. So we regard these laws — we presume that what the legislature has done is constitutional.

There are two categories of cases, Stone suggested, where that's not the right approach. One is when fundamental liberties, when the guarantees of the Bill of Rights are at stake, First Amendment rights are at stake. The Court is the guardian of the Bill of Rights, and it should see to it that Congress remembers that Congress is to pass no law abridging the freedom of speech or of the press. The other category: cases where the majority was disadvantaging the minority. So then you really couldn't trust the political process. The minority that was being oppressed didn't have the political clout; you couldn't trust the majority to deal fairly with them — what was suspect was the majority disadvantaging the minority. And over time, race has become the suspect criterion. When a state university wants to have an affirmative action plan of the most moderate kind, who is the Court to say that's unconstitutional? Again, it's being deferential to another decision maker.

JR: You sound once again like you're being a better originalist than Justice Scalia. We have two cases involving affirmative action where you're saying, in fact, the constitutional history is on your side, and you're a champion of respecting original understanding and of judicial restraint.

RBG: The *Carolene Products* footnote was an insight that the Court had. You know, some people think that suspect classification started with the *Korematsu* case [in 1944]. But it's back there in the days when the Court stopped putting down social and economic legislation and recognized that, for the most part, the legislature should not be put down. The question is, who decides what is good social and economic policy? Not the Court, but the legislature. *Carolene Products* was such a case — a typical economic regulation case, and the Court said what Congress did was okay. Then Stone added a qualification: maybe sometimes we have to be more suspicious about what Congress is doing.

JR: That's what the Court said during the New Deal era, but you suggested in your health care dissent on the Commerce Clause point that perhaps some members of the Court were trying to resurrect the battles of economic judicial activism. In the health care case, you said that the attempt to strike down the individual mandate of the Affordable Care Act under the Commerce Clause had resurrections of *Lochner v. New York,* that infamous case from the Progressive Era that struck down maximum hours laws for bakers. Are you afraid of a resurrection of economic judicial activism along these lines?

RBG: It seemed to me that the Affordable Care Act was just the completion of what was started in the thirties with Social Security. The Social Security Act was upheld by the Court, and many people thought after that, the Court was recognizing that economic and social policy was not its domain, so if the legislature wants to pass a minimum wage law, a maximum hours law, that was the legislature's prerogative. Most countries in the world, most industrialized countries, have universal health care. They had Social Security long before we did. So I saw the health care act as just completing that flaw, that safety net — people will have Social Security coverage when they're elderly or when a partner dies, and health care should be part of that same understanding, that government does have an obligation to see that people's basic needs are met.

But I understand the resistance. The Social Security Act — the name of the ACT is FICA, the Federal Insurance Contributions Act. Well, it was sold to the public as an earned right. Work, you pay an insurance premium, but you are not paying an insurance premium at all. You're paying a tax, pure and simple. That's what Social Security is. It's a tax we pay so that people who are no longer able to work will be taken care of. I thought once the Social Security Act was accepted, there would be no question anymore about the Commerce Clause extending to health care.

The truth about health care — it was portrayed as taking the young and the healthy and making them pay for the elderly and the infirm. But if you think of a person over the span of time — so today you are young and healthy. In the not-too-distant future, you will be middle-aged, and then you will be old, and then there will be young people who are paying for you. So if you look at it as a whole life span, yes, you're paying a tax when you are young, and the state is providing services you don't need. But over the long run it evens out.

JR: Of course, the question of whether it was or wasn't a tax proved to be central, and there was some comedy about it during the debates. All the Democrats stood up and said, "It's not a tax," and the Republicans said, "It is." And as soon as the ink was dry, they switched, and all the Democrats said, "It definitely is a tax and is therefore constitutional," and the Republicans said, "It's not a tax and therefore isn't justified by the taxing power."

RBG: But that was — that does reflect the debate at the time of Social Security. Social Security was a tax. It was not an insurance premium, but it was sold as not a tax. And even our president tried to sell the health care by calling it not a tax. It was a penalty.

JR: Penalty, yes. Should that matter, what the president called it? I mean, it proved not to be dispositive.

RBG: I mean, the president wanted to get the health care act through Congress, and there was a very strong view that — no more taxes, we will not enact any more taxes, so call it a penalty.

JR: What did you think of the chief justice's

decision to uphold it as a tax?

RBG: Oh, I thought it was interesting that although he saw the Commerce Clause as limited, he saw the Tax Clause as expansive. Congress can tax as it will, and it's not hemmed in by — how could anyone think that health insurance doesn't involve commerce? Think of the criticism today of the health care act. It is said, in some quarters, that it will be the ruination of small business. Well, small business is commerce, right? It is very difficult to understand how that cutback on the reach of the Commerce Clause came about. I think it will not have staying power.

JR: What do you mean? It will be overturned?

RBG: That view, yes. And we will get back to where we were ever since the late thirties, when economic and social legislation is recognized as the proper domain of the Congress, and that, as devoted as you may be to your particular state, there are so many things in this highly industrialized world that states can't do, that have to have a national solution.

JR: That point about the national solution was another example of you being a good originalist, because you said that the framers of the Constitution were concerned about the collective action problems in the Articles of Confederation, and wanted to empower Congress to act when the states were powerless to coordinate their actions together. So you do believe the Commerce Clause reading will be overturned eventually. Are you concerned in the short term that it might lead to invalidation of other economic legislation, environmental laws, health and safety laws, and so forth?

RBG: I'm hopeful that it will not have that ramification. All of the precedent, except this health care decision, is the other way.

JR: Let me ask now about the marriage equality cases, about the Defense of Marriage Act case [*United States v. Windsor*] and *Hollingsworth v. Perry*. In the DOMA case, you found that there was standing to hear the case, and in the *Perry* case, that there was not standing. What was the difference between the two?

RBG: There was standing in both cases originally. In the Defense of Marriage Act case — I think you know the background of the case that the Court decided. These were two people who lived together in a loving partnership, and one of them was dying and wanted to have the official blessings of government on their union, so they married in Canada and then came back to New York, which recognizes gay marriage and recognized the Canadian marriage. And then the one partner died, and the other gets something like a $360,000 estate tax bill from the government. She would have no bill at all if her marriage were recognized; she would get the marital deduction. So that was the DOMA case. Originally, the government was defending the law, as it ordinarily does, but then it decided, after the case was heard in the court of first instance, that the plaintiff was right, and the law was indeed unconstitutional.

So one would think that would render the case moot, except that although the government switched sides in its view of what the Constitution required, it didn't give the surviving spouse her refund. So as long as the government was holding the money, there was a continuing case or controversy. It was on that basis that the Court said, yes, we can hear the case. It's still a live case or controversy; she hasn't gotten the refund.

And if you're concerned about will the Court be given the best arguments on both sides? Well, surely that was so. I think we had over a hundred friend-of-the-court briefs in the DOMA case. We were very well informed of everyone's views on this. So, you had the adversary presentations, and you had a controversy that was not yet over.

JR: I was in the courtroom for the DOMA case and remember that remarkable moment when Justice Kagan read from the House report, which said, "Congress decided to reflect and honor collective moral judgment and to express moral disapproval of homosexuality." There was a gasp in the courtroom when she read that. Was the case over from that moment? Because the Court has said that moral disapproval is not a legitimate basis for laws under even relaxed scrutiny.

RBG: Some people, as you know, say we should look at the text of the laws that Congress passes, and we should not pay any attention at all to so-called legislative history, what they say on the floor, even what they say in committee reports. So, that kind of statement, which was startling — that this was an expression of moral disapproval

— that would have no influence on someone who doesn't look at legislative history.

JR: Now, that "some people" who don't like legislative history includes, most prominently, Justice Scalia, of course. And you had called Justice Scalia to task for having objected to judicial activism in the Defense of Marriage Act case but not being reluctant to strike down an act of Congress in the Voting Rights Act case.

RBG: Yes, even without the legislative history, where there were reams of legislative history showing the continuing need for the Voting Rights Act.

JR: So perhaps that's the answer to my questions about what's the difference between these cases? The Defense of Marriage Act case is one case where you did vote to invalidate an act of Congress, which you earlier defined as judicial activism. Why was it okay to strike down the Defense of Marriage Act but not the Voting Rights Act?

RBG: Because the Defense of Marriage Act was Congress violating the equality and liberty guarantees. That fell in what I would call Justice Stone's first category. The Court has to be careful to see that Congress is not treading on our most fundamental human values. DOMA wasn't the first time the Court encountered this question. It wasn't so long ago that many states made consensual sodomy a crime. And the Court, at first, in *Bowers v. Hardwick,* said that's okay, it's okay to express moral disapproval of that kind of activity. And then the Court turned around in the *Lawrence* case and said the state has no business intruding on the lives of people who are doing something that doesn't harm anyone. And then there was the Colorado ordinance case after that. So the Court had already . . . the themes that were expressed in DOMA had already been sounded.

JR: And there was also, of course, the Virginia Military Institute case, which you wrote so eloquently, that said that preserving tradition for its own sake is also not a legitimate purpose. That sort of knocked out the reasons people had for opposing same-sex marriage, and made the case perhaps easier for the challengers.

You famously, and I think persuasively, argued that the Court overreached in *Roe v. Wade,* and that had it merely struck down the Texas law at issue in the case and not settled abortion for the whole nation, it might have avoided the backlash that ended up harming abortion rights. What is the difference between marriage equality and abortion? Why was the Court not jumping ahead of public opinion in this case in a way that you think it did do in *Roe v. Wade*?

RBG: The Court is a reactive institution. You react to the controversies that are brought to the Court. In DOMA, it was a couple claiming that their marriage had the same right to be recognized by government as anyone else's. So the only way that case could be resolved is by saying DOMA, which says that these people will be treated by the federal government as not married, is unconstitutional.

10
MEASURED MOTIONS

For most of her career on the bench, Ruth Bader Ginsburg was known as a judge's judge, a judicial minimalist who believed that social change comes slowly and from the ground up, fired by political activism, ratified by Congress and state legislatures, and, only after that, carried forward by courts. And the best way to understand Ginsburg's restrained view of the judicial function is to read her many articles and speeches on the subject before and after she was nominated to the Supreme Court.

Her Madison Lecture at New York University in 1992 got the most attention for its criticisms of *Roe v. Wade.* But the lecture is also significant in defending what Ginsburg calls "measured motions" by courts that have faced demands for social change throughout American history. "The Justices generally follow, they do not lead, changes taking place elsewhere in society," Ginsburg wrote. "But without taking giant strides and thereby risking a backlash too forceful to contain, the Court, through constitutional adjudication, can reinforce or signal a green light for a social change." She discusses the sex discrimination cases she had argued in the 1970s, where she asked the Court to add its weight to an already evident social change rather than leading it. "In most of the post-1970 gender-classification cases, unlike *Roe,* the Court . . . approved the direction of change through a temperate brand of decision-making, one that was not extravagant or divisive. *Roe,* on the other hand, halted a political process that was moving in a reform direction and thereby, I believe, prolonged divisiveness and deferred stable settlement of the issue."[1]

But Ginsburg also recognized that there are times when the Court has to step ahead of the political branches. In the case of gender discrimination, women were able to enlighten their husbands and sons about the need for gender equality once their own consciousness was awakened. In the case of race discrimination, by contrast, "when blacks were confined by law to a separate sector, there was no similar prospect for educating the white majority."[2] Because there was little prospect of state legislatures dismantling segregation in the South, the Court in *Brown v. Board of Education* had to step into the breach. Still, Ginsburg stressed, "it was not an altogether bold decision," for two reasons. "First, Thurgood Marshall and those who worked with him in the campaign against racial injustice, carefully set the stepping stones leading up to the landmark ruling." And second, instead of launching a "broadside attack" on Jim Crow in all its manifestations, the Court "concentrated on segregated schools; it left the follow-up for other days and future cases." It wasn't until the civil rights movement of the 1960s, "which *Brown* helped to propel" and which culminated in the Civil Rights Act of 1964, that the Court was ultimately ready for the "total rejection of Jim Crow legislation." By the time the Court struck down state bans on interracial marriages in *Loving v. Virginia* in 1967, Ginsburg notes, the Court "effectively ruled that, with regard to racial classifications, the doctrine of 'separate but equal' was dead."[3]

Ginsburg set out her restrained view of the relationship between the courts and social change soon after she joined the appellate bench. In a 1981 article, "Inviting Judicial Activism: A 'Liberal' or 'Conservative' Technique?" she endorsed "a principled, appropriately restrained approach for the courts," namely: "There should be no intrusion into the affairs of a coequal branch on the invitation of a legislator when collective action by the Congress would afford the individual plaintiffs significant relief."[4] She commented on a 1971 memo, little noticed at the time, in which the future Supreme Court justice Lewis Powell told the U.S. Chamber of Commerce that "the judiciary may be the most important instrument for social, economic and political change." As Ginsburg put it, Powell "advised the business community to adopt the 'astute' ways of activist liberals 'in exploiting judicial action.' "[5] In the years since Powell's memo, Ginsburg observed, "public interest legal foundations have been established to represent 'conservative' or business interests" — including the Mountain States Legal Foundation and the Pacific Legal Foundation, "both regular challengers in court, often in opposition to consumer and environmental groups."[6] Today, the most open calls for "judicial engagement," as libertarian conservatives now call it, comes in briefs filed by those pro-business advocacy groups, supported by the litigation group of the U.S. Chamber of Commerce, which in 2008 won thirteen out of the fifteen cases in which it filed briefs, the highest percentage in the group's thirty-year history.[7] In one of those cases, Ginsburg filed the sole dissent.[8] But other pro-business cases were nearly unanimous, such as *Skilling v. United States,* in 2010, where Ginsburg wrote the opinion for the Court, reversing the conviction of the former Enron executive Jeffrey Skilling for conspiring to defraud Enron shareholders by misrepresenting the company's value because his conduct didn't involve bribes or kickbacks.

One of the most important disputes on the Supreme Court today is about what kind of limits the Constitution imposes on Congress's ability to delegate the power to regulate the economy to administrative entities such as the Environmental Protection Agency or the Food and Drug Administration. The *Citizens United* case held, over Justice Ginsburg's dissent, that corporations have the same First Amendment rights as natural persons. And now some libertarians and conservatives who are skeptical of federal regulations are urging the Supreme Court to overturn a 1984 case called *Chevron v. Natural Resources Defense Council,* which requires judges to defer to interpretations of ambiguous federal laws made by the agencies in charge of enforcing them, unless the interpretations are clearly unreasonable. According to *Chevron,* courts must generally uphold health and safety regulations unless they obviously conflict with what Congress intended.

Today, Justice Neil Gorsuch has become the most prominent judicial critic of *Chevron,* on the grounds that it violates the separation of powers by permitting "executive bureaucracies to swallow huge amounts of core judicial and legislative power."[9] Gorsuch and other justices are encouraging courts to scrutinize federal regulations more closely, in ways that, as Ginsburg warned in 1981, could encourage courts rather than Congress to supervise administrative agencies.[10] This call for judicial restraint is in keeping with her principled belief that social change should come from legislatures rather than courts, a belief that led her to strike down fewer federal, state, and local laws between 1994 and 2001 than any other justice.[11]

JR: When you think about your constitutional legacy, who's your model?

RBG: I couldn't identify one model. There are several. Certainly, the great chief justice John Marshall, who made the Court what it is today. You remember that John Jay, when he was elected governor of New York, thought that was a better job than chief justice. When George Washington wanted Jay to return to the chief justice's seat, Jay said no, the Court will never amount to much. Marshall made the Court an independent third branch of the government, so he is certainly a hero. Another justice, one who didn't serve very long — six years, I think — was Justice Benjamin Curtis, who wrote a fine dissent in the *Dred Scott* case. Sometime later, the first Justice John Marshall Harlan, who dissented in *Plessy v. Ferguson.* Further along, of course, Brandeis and Holmes and their great dissents, mainly in the free speech area but also in dissenting opinions explaining that social and economic legislation should be left largely to legislators and should not be second-guessed by the Court. And then, of course, Thurgood Marshall.

JR: In thinking about the Constitution and change when it comes to civil liberties, how and why does the Court come to change its mind?

RBG: Society changes. If it didn't, we would not have had a chance to prevail in the cases of the 1970s. Women were doing all kinds of things. Doors were open to them. There were very few occupations where women were not welcome. And as more women were out there doing things, it encouraged young women to believe, well, this is what I want, and I can do it. The Court, a great legal scholar once said, should never be affected by the weather of the day. But inevitably, it will be affected by the climate of the era. One classic example of that is *Brown v. Board of Education.* We had not long before fought a war against racism, against the Nazis' persecution and torture and murder of Jews. And yet our own troops, in the Second World War, were segregated by race. Some people thought there was something terribly wrong with that. We were proclaiming that racism is odious, and yet we were practicing it ourselves. So I think that the time, the change, people realizing how wrong it was to maintain racial barriers — it was the climate of that time that gave the impetus, I think, for *Brown v. Board.*

JR: How can the justices know when social change represents the climate of the era rather than the weather of the day?

RBG: It's all around us, it's what our neighbors are doing, what our children are doing, what the press is reporting. It's inescapable. To go back to *Brown,* a concern the United States government had was definitely part of the picture. At that time, we were in a Cold War with the Soviet Union, and the State Department filed a brief in *Brown v. Board* urging the Court to end what was basically apartheid in America. It said, we are being embarrassed constantly by the Soviet Union charging that the United States is a racist society. Please, Court, help us to end that era.

JR: And yet sometimes the justices move too fast. You have argued that *Roe v. Wade* was too broad when it came down, that the social change was in the middle of unfolding, and if the Court had moved more narrowly, then reproductive rights might have been protected politically.

RBG: Yes.

JR: This theme of when the Court should intervene and when it should pull back comes up in the death penalty cases — juvenile death penalty and the mentally challenged. Should you just count up the number of states that embrace a certain practice and, if more than half of them have done something, ratify that?

RBG: That's not what the Court has been doing. On the death penalty, there was a time — how many years was it between *Furman* and *Gregg* [respectively, the decision that invalidated state death penalty laws and the decision that provided guidelines for reinstating them]?

JR: Nineteen seventy-two to 1976. It wasn't a long time. It was a few years.

RBG: The Supreme Court had struck down the death penalty, recognizing that it wasn't being administered with an even hand. No account was taken of mitigating circumstances. And there were no standards for deciding who would live and who would die. For some years, there were no executions in the country. Then states began to change their laws to set standards. It's not your everyday murderer that gets the death penalty. It has to be a heinous, cruel, atrocious murder. The worst of the worst fit that category. Then states returned to the Supreme Court, urging: we now have standards, so let us say for ourselves whether we want the death penalty. The Supreme Court looked at the standards and responded, "Okay, you can have it." If the Supreme Court had not decided as it did in 1976, we likely would have no death penalty today, and it wouldn't even be controversial.

JR: The danger of backlash is one of your themes. There's a real danger of backlash. But when I teach constitutional law, I always begin by telling students, "Don't imagine it's all politics. If you jump right to that conclusion, then you'll miss everything that's beautiful and constraining and mean-ingful about the Constitution." But we see numbers like this, and you talk about Justice O'Connor being replaced by Justice Alito, and I have to ask: Is it all politics in these high-profile cases? Republicans against Democrats?

RBG: Well, I think all of us would answer no, the Court is not a political branch of government. Many times, I will vote for or write an opinion that would not be the law if I were queen. Yes, we see our fundamental instrument of government differently, but there's certainly no horse trading at the Court: if you vote for me today, I'll vote for you tomorrow. That never happens. But we do hold some very different views.

Let's take the Fourteenth Amendment's Equal Protection Clause, for example. Today the equal protection guarantee extends to women, but if you ask the question "Back in 1868, when the Fourteenth Amendment became part of the Constitution, did the people at that time envision that women would be citizens equal in stature to men?" The answer, surely no. But as I see the equality idea — it was there from the beginning and was realized by society over time. So I would say this: It's true that in 1868 women were a long way from having the vote. But then the Nineteenth Amendment was ratified in 1920, and women gained the vote. We had the civil rights movement of the 1960s aimed at making the equality guarantee real for race — as it should have been from the beginning. Those developments inform my view of what the Equal Protection Clause means today.

JR: As an advocate, you slowly built a consensus for women's equality at a time when this was hotly contested in the country. Do you take from this experience that the Court should be careful not to jump too far ahead — that it should maybe nudge, but generally follow, rather than lead?

RBG: I don't know an age in which the Court has really led. Let's return to *Brown v. Board,* probably the most celebrated decision of the twentieth century, and rightly so. But it wasn't just Thurgood Marshall's great advocacy and his careful plan working up to *Brown.* It was the aftermath of World War II; we had just fought a war against odious racism, and yet our own troops were separated by race.

I was tremendously fortunate to be born at the right time and to be in the right place. Women generations before said the same things my generation was saying, but they did so at a time when no one, or precious few, were prepared to listen.

JR: You've been called, admiringly, a judicial minimalist. Do you think the Court should always take baby steps, even when it's reflecting social change, basically nudging or catching up, but not really pushing too hard?

RBG: No, sometimes the Court must be more assertive. For example, in the aftermath of *Brown v. Board,* there was out-and-out refusal to follow the law of the land. It was not just the Supreme Court that remained firm. Much more so it was the judges in the trenches, in the trial courts, in the Courts of Appeals, who insisted that the law of the land is no law-enforced separation of the races in schools. The very lives of some of those judges were in danger, but they enforced the decision.

JR: *Brown v. Board* is still hotly contested today, as people argue whether the Equal Protection Clause requires color blindness or color consciousness. What does *Brown* mean today, and is there actually agreement about the core meaning of *Brown*?

RBG: The culmination of the civil rights cases that led up to *Brown* came thirteen years later, in 1967, in *Loving v. Virginia*. The Lovings grew up in a rural area of Virginia where people got along with each other. Racial differences didn't disturb their neighborliness. Mildred [Jeter], an African American, and Richard Loving, a Caucasian, met, fell in love, and went to DC to get married because interracial marriage was banned in Virginia. Marriage license in hand, they returned to Virginia. One night, the sheriff came to their home, blared his flashlight on them, and commanded, *Get out of bed and come with me to see the judge.* They pointed to their marriage certificate, which they had framed and posted on their bedroom wall. *That doesn't count for anything here,* the sheriff barked. The judge said he would not sentence them to prison if they agreed to leave the state of Virginia and never come back together. The civil rights movement and Martin Luther King were becoming prominent in our land. Mildred Loving, like Sally Reed, was an everyday person. But she thought that maybe there was hope that the system would work for her this time. The case was eventually argued before the Supreme Court and ended in a unanimous decision. With *Loving v. Virginia,* official apartheid in America ended.

JR: Today, the debate about judicial activism focuses on whether this is a pro-business Supreme Court. That is what the progressives are all saying, and they note that the U.S. Chamber of Commerce has won the overwhelming majority of its cases, 81 percent. Now, you are among the least consistently pro-business justices, according to the surveys, voting for the Chamber's position less than anyone else, only 35 percent of the time. Is this a fair charge, and is this a pro-business Court?

RBG: I thought you were going to ask me how could I let Jeffrey Skilling off the hook in the Enron case? In his case, the Chamber of Commerce took a position with which all nine of us agreed. Congress had written a statute making it a crime to deprive another of "honest services." The term "honest services" was so vague it could not define a criminal offense. I don't regard myself as pro-business, or anti-business; I just call them as they come as best as I can.

JR: There's another trope, and that's the old debate about activism and restraint. And here's another statistic: you are the most restrained justice, if restraint is defined in the traditional way of simply striking down state and federal laws. Between 1994 and 2001, you were the justice least likely to strike down federal, state, or local laws. Isn't it an odd world where suddenly restraint has been redefined, and you're called an activist if you don't strike down health care or economic reform or campaign finance reform?

RBG: The label "activist," what does it

mean? Nowadays, does it not mean, whose ox is being gored? In the kind of score you posited, who has voted to strike down more federal, state, local legislation? Justice Scalia should have been high up on the list of activist judges, if that's how you measure it.

JR: He was number two, the second most activist, as you said. This is the same debate that we're engaging in right now, that was going on in the Progressive Era, when the liberals were saying, "This is a pro-business Court," and the conservatives were saying, "You have to strike down progressive laws, and strike down the New Deal." Might we — this is obviously a serious question; answer it as you can — might we see a resurrection of those New Deal battles, where the Supreme Court, by divided votes, is challenging the president and Congress on issues they care intensely about?

RBG: I think that era is long over. Even my colleagues who might have some doubts, if it were decades earlier, are prepared to recognize the proper role of the legislature in social and economic legislation. So, no, I don't think there will be a return to the Court of the 1920s and early 1930s. And I can say with some confidence I don't think there will be another court-packing plan, either. Franklin Delano Roosevelt was so annoyed by the nine old men who kept striking down state and federal economic and social legislation. But he couldn't fire the justices, because we hold our offices during "good behavior" — that's what the Constitution says. So his proposal was for every justice who turned seventy and a half years old, a new justice could be appointed. That would have given him, immediately, six appointments, and the Court would have swelled in size from nine to fifteen. I don't think we are in any great danger of that happening again.

JR: What about the skepticism of several of the justices toward the *Chevron* doctrine, which suggests that the administrative state may be in for a rough ride?

RBG: One of the justices is already on record for the view that *Chevron* was wrong and should be overturned. I remember years ago — it's funny how things turn full circle. In the 1980s there was some support for a measure known as the Bumpers Amendment, named for its sponsor, Senator Dale Bumpers of Arkansas. That measure would have required the Court to give no deference to an agency's reading of the statute it administered. I don't know what combination of forces kept the Bumpers Amendment from passing. But it's interesting that the Bumpers Amendment was pushed by a Democrat and now the other side is embracing the position.

JR: But should citizens be concerned about these challenges to the administrative state? What is at stake?

RBG: Such is the nature of our society. There are so many matters that must be handled on the federal level. The administrative state is not going to disappear. *Chevron* isn't all that old. If truth be told, I wrote the DC Circuit decision striking the regulation the Supreme Court upheld when it announced the *Chevron* doctrine.

JR: Ah! But the doctrine wasn't in place, so you didn't know it would prompt that decision.

RBG: The DC Circuit had reached to a compromise in prior decisions. The EPA could put strict requirements on dirty-air areas, but the still-clean areas could not be put under this same stringent regime.

Anyway, Justice Stevens, who wrote the Court's opinion in *Chevron,* acknowledged that I was following circuit precedent. We had an administrative state long before *Chevron,* and it will remain, whatever the fate of *Chevron.*

11
#MeToo and a More Perfect Union

Like most people, Justice Ginsburg did not predict the meteoric rise of the #MeToo movement, which burst into the public consciousness in October 2017, when the *New York Times* reported that film producer Harvey Weinstein was being accused by several women of sexual misconduct spanning three decades. The actress Ashley Judd was one of the first to gain attention. In several of our conversations, Ginsburg celebrated the movement, which she believes will have staying power because it helps men as well as women understand how sexual misconduct subordinates women. At the same time, she emphasized the importance of due process for the accuser as well as the accused.

For Ginsburg, the #MeToo movement, like the gay rights movement and the feminist movement of the 1970s, is an example of how quickly social change can be produced by political activism from the ground up. In her view, legal change follows social and political change, not the other way around. The Equal Pay Act of 1963 and Title VII of the Civil Rights Act of 1964, for example, reflected the social changes of the post–World War II era, an "unprecedent[ed] growth . . . in the employment of women," she wrote, precipitated by "a sharp decline in necessary home-centered activity, curtailed population goals and more effective means of controlling reproduction, and vastly extended life spans."[1] As Ginsburg has emphasized, it was the sheer number of women entering the workforce that changed the ways in which men and women interacted. Quoting the sociologist Cynthia Epstein, she stressed men's need to learn about equality "when women show up in their midst in numbers, not as one-at-a-time curiosities, or only in subordinate, helping roles. Men need the experience of working with women who display a wide range of personality characteristics. They need to become working friends with women."[2] Noting Bureau of Labor Statistics reports from the late 1970s projecting that, by 1992, "two-thirds of all women age twenty-five to fifty-four will be in the paid labor force" (in fact, the proportion in 2019 is just 57 percent), Ginsburg insisted that technological and infrastructural changes were less important than women's participation in the workforce in defining the "guts of a society" — "how it works and plays, how people relate to one another, whether they have children, and how they bring them up."[3]

For Ginsburg, the #MeToo movement is a vindication of the vision of feminism that she championed in the 1970s: a rejection of the traditional idea that women and men occupy separate spheres in which women are naturally passive and men aggressive; an attack on laws treating men and women differently, especially those designed to protect "the weaker sex"; and an insistence that special benefits for women be extended to men.

In the 1980s, however, Ginsburg's vision of gender equality came under bitter attack by a new generation of feminist legal scholars who argued that the law should emphasize women's differences from men, rather than their similarities. The new feminists called Ginsburg "phallocentric" and "assimilationist" for challenging classifications that burdened men as well as women and for mostly representing male plaintiffs. "As applied, the sameness standard has mostly gotten men the benefit of those few things women have historically had — for all the good they did us,"[4] wrote the legal scholar Catharine MacKinnon in 1984.

Rather than seeking legal equality, MacKinnon argued, feminists should target instead the broader evil of social structures that "devalue" women. Accordingly, the feminists of the 1980s sought to resurrect many of the special protections for women that Ginsburg had opposed, from sweeping bans on pornography to child-rearing benefits for mothers but not fathers. The unexpected debate among feminists about whether Ginsburg's advocacy hurt more than it helped women brings to mind Malcolm X's attacks on Thurgood Marshall for being insufficiently black. It also explained some of the ambivalence within the women's movement when Ginsburg was nominated to the Court.[5]

Ginsburg's public responses to her feminist critics were typically circumspect. She called the charge of assimilationism "not fair," adding that "the litigation of the 1970s helped unsettle previously accepted conceptions of men's and women's separate spheres." But she could not conceal her hurt feelings when some of her feminist successors failed to appreciate her achievements.

"I am concerned about a threat to women achievers not only from men who are insecure, and whose insecurity causes them to fear women who do not shrink — or pretend to defer — when a male voice speaks," she said in a 1984 speech. She added, "I am concerned too about women, some of them feminists, who seem to have joined the attack by condemning their sisters."[6] Opposing "special favors" for women (such as part-time judgeships for women with young children), Ginsburg endorsed instead day-care centers for both sexes supported by private employers and the federal government.

The great irony of the debate about special treatment versus equal treatment for women, as Ginsburg noted, is that the "separate modes thesis" of the new legal feminists looks very much like "the old typology in which the female is classified in terms of passion and its bonds, the male in terms of reason and its distinctions." And it was this typology of difference that had been used to justify the legal subordination of women until the 1970s. Most laws that drew an explicit distinction between men and women, as Ginsburg noted, did so ostensibly to protect women, or "benignly prefer" them. Laws prescribing the maximum number of hours women, but not men, could work; laws excluding women from "hazardous" occupations such as bartending; even laws requiring men but not women to serve on juries — all used the rhetoric of "separate but equal" to conceal their assumption that women could not fend for themselves.

"I am fearful, or suspicious, of generalizations about the way women or men are," Ginsburg said repeatedly in the 1980s. "My life's experience indicates that they cannot guide me reliably in making decisions about particular individuals." She quoted the sociologist Cynthia Epstein for the proposition that "human caring and concern, for home, children, and the welfare of others, ought not be regarded as dominantly 'women's work,' it should become the work of all."[7]

Ginsburg was prophetic in recognizing that even with formally equal opportunities, women could be held back by what she called as early as the 1970s "unconscious bias." In a 1978 article on seemingly benign sex classifications, she cited a case in which white male managers consistently chose white males for promotion at the New York Telephone Company by invoking a standard they called the "total person concept."[8] And in a 1999 lecture, she noted with approval

237

Marschall v. Land Nordrhein-Westfalen, a 1997 decision by the European Court of Justice that upheld a German law that made gender the tiebreaker in civil service promotions, favoring women but allowing a man to prevail over a woman, despite the tiebreaker, if specific factors tilted the balance in his favor. Comparing the decision to Justice Lewis Powell's opinion in the *Bakke* case, which upheld Harvard's affirmative action program that used race as a plus factor rather than the decisive factor, Ginsburg stressed the importance of rooting out unconscious bias. "The decision in *Marschall* is perhaps most notable for its sensitivity to sometimes unconscious bias," she wrote, noting that traditional male employers might wrongly fear that women would be distracted from their work by stereotypical family duties. "A tie-breaker preference for women may do no more than ensure actual adherence to the nondiscrimination principle. Without such positive action by government, unconscious or half-conscious discrimination might continue unchecked."[9]

At the end of the 1970s, as Ginsburg concluded her days as an advocate, the largest piece of unfinished business that concerned her was the Supreme Court's rejection of the idea that the Constitution prohibited unconscious bias on the basis of sex. In what Ginsburg called a "significant loss," in 1979 the Court, in *Personnel Administration of Massachusetts v. Feeney,* upheld a lifetime, top-of-the-list preference in Massachusetts for veterans applying for civil service jobs. Given that almost all veterans at the time were men, Ginsburg noted soon after the decision "the extreme preference concededly had a devastating impact on employment opportunities for women." Nevertheless, the Court held that the Constitution prohibits only intentional discrimination on the basis of sex, not discrimination infected by unconscious bias that has an adverse impact on women. "*Feeney* indicates that when a classification is neutral in form and is drawn for a laudable purpose," Ginsburg lamented, "the Court will allow the measure to stand without modification although its adverse impact on one sex is severe and inevitable."[10]

For Ginsburg, therefore, the #MeToo movement, in which women used social media and other platforms to demand the same respect in the workplace as their male colleagues, was a vindication of her vision that women should empower themselves by joining the workplace in numbers and refusing to tolerate unequal treatment, intentional or unintentional. Ginsburg believes that the Constitution should be interpreted to root out unconscious biases that subordinate women. But as she recognized decades ago, true equality requires that men and women work together to root out unconscious bias in families and in the workplace. "My dream for my children and their children," she said in 1984, "is of men and women who, in combination, forge new, shared patterns of career and parenthood, and strive to create a society that facilitates those patterns."[11]

JR: What are your thoughts on the #MeToo movement, and will it prove lasting progress for women's equality?

RBG: Sexual harassment of women has gone on forever, but it didn't get headlines until a woman named Catharine MacKinnon wrote a book called *Sexual Harassment of Working Women,* and that was the start of litigation under Title VII [of the Civil Rights Act]. A few cases came to the Supreme Court, and women prevailed. But still, women were hesitant.

A principal reason for the hesitancy was that women feared they would not be believed. The number of women who have come forward as a result of the #MeToo movement has been astonishing. My hope is not just that it is here to stay, but that it is as effective for the woman who works as a maid in a hotel as it is for Hollywood stars.

JR: Many women are wondering, will this prove a lasting advance for women or, like previous discussions of sexual harassment in the nineties, will this advance pass?

RBG: I think it will have staying power because people, and not only women — men as well as women — realize how wrong the behavior was and how it subordinated women. So, we shall see, but my prediction is that it is here to stay.

JR: Why is it happening now? Is there something about what millennials are doing that has caused the #MeToo movement, or is it something else?

RBG: I think we can compare it to the gay rights movement, when people stepped up and said, "This is who I am, and I am proud of it." They came out in numbers instead of hiding, disguising. That movement developed very rapidly, and I think we are seeing the same thing with sexual harassment.

JR: Did you see this one coming?

RBG: No. And why did it happen just when it did? I've heard from women who told stories about Harvey Weinstein many years ago. And then, one fine day, the *Times* decided to do a big story on it. I think it was the press finally reporting something they knew long before that propelled #MeToo to the place it now holds in the public arena.

JR: What is your advice to all women about how to sustain the momentum of the movement and to make its changes lasting?

RBG: I have heard from lawyers about women coming forward with reports of things that happened many years ago, even though the statute of limitations is long past. These cases are being settled. One interesting question is whether we will see an end to the confidentiality pledge. Women who complained and brought suit were offered settlements in which they would agree that they would never disclose what they had complained about. I hope those agreements will not be enforced by courts.

JR: What are the legal changes necessary to make these reforms permanent?

RBG: We have the legal reforms; we have had them for a long time. Title VII. It was argued early on that sexual harassment has nothing to do with gender discrimination. Everyone knows boys will be boys, and that was that. There are state and federal laws proscribing harassment. The laws are there, the laws are in place; it takes people to step forward and use them.

JR: You've told your own #MeToo story, about an encounter at Cornell long ago.

RBG: I was in a chemistry class at Cornell. I was not very adept in the laboratory, so a teaching assistant decided to help me out. He offered to give me a practice exam the day before the actual exam. The next day, I picked up the actual exam paper and found that it was identical to the practice exam. I knew immediately what this instructor expected as a payoff. So, instead of being shy, I confronted him and said, "How dare you do this?" That is one of many, many stories every woman of my vintage can tell.

JR: What would you advise women to say

243

in a similar situation? Should they be similarly strong?

RBG: Yes. Say, "This is bad behavior. You should not engage in it, and I will not submit to it." But I think it is easier today because there are numbers to support the woman who says so. We no longer hear as often as we did in the past, "She's making it up."

JR: What is your advice to men in this new regime where people are trying to behave well and figure out what the new norms are?

RBG: Just think how you would like the women in your family to be treated, particularly your daughters. And when you see men behaving in ways they should not, you should tell them this is improper behavior.

JR: Can men become more enlightened?

RBG: Well, I think you can answer that for yourself.

JR: You are wiser than I am. It is a very important question.

RBG: You can see what happened in the

seventies. Up until then, the Supreme Court never saw a gender-based classification it didn't like or regarded as unconstitutional.

JR: There is a debate both among women and among men about what sort of behavior should be sanctionable, and one group is saying that it's wrong to lump together violent behavior like Harvey Weinstein's with less dramatic forms of sexual misconduct, and others say that all misconduct is wrong and should be sanctioned.

RBG: Well, there are degrees of conduct, yes. But anytime a woman is put in a position where she is made to feel inferior, subordinate, there should be — she should complain, she should not be afraid.

JR: What about due process for the accused?

RBG: Well, that must not be ignored, and it goes beyond sexual harassment. The person who is accused has a right to defend herself or himself, and we certainly should not lose sight of that, at the same time recognizing that these are complaints that should be heard. There's been criticism of some college codes of conduct for not giving the accused person a fair opportunity to be heard. That's one of the basic tenets of our system, as you know: everyone deserves a fair hearing.

JR: Are some of those criticisms of the college codes valid?

RBG: Do I think they are? Yes.

JR: I think people are hungry for your thoughts about how to balance the values of due process against the need for increased gender equality.

RBG: It's not one or the other. It's both. We have a system of justice where people who are accused are entitled to due process. So one must apply to this field what we have applied generally.

JR: Some women also fear backlash. They worry that women may have less opportunity for mentorship at work because guys are afraid of interacting with them. Is this valid or not?

RBG: Well, let me ask you: As a man, do you think you will be hesitant to encourage women because of the #MeToo movement?

JR: On the contrary, I have felt, like many men, sensitized to the plight of women by hearing these stories, and it seems like an entirely salutary thing.

RBG: Yes.

JR: You've said that the courts are the least important part of social change. First comes political activism and public education, and then legislation, and then the courts. So, looking forward ten or twenty years, how does the momentum of the #MeToo movement get reflected in legislation and in judicial decisions?

RBG: As I said, I think the law is there, and people will use it in increasing numbers. But rights have to start with people who want them. The court is a reactive institution. There was a fine federal judge on the Fifth Circuit, Judge Irving Goldberg, who once said, "The courts don't make the conflagrations, but they do their best to put them out."

JR: In 1986, you wrote an essay in which you said the following: "My principal affirmative action plan would have three legs. First, it would promote equal educational opportunity, effective job training for women. Second, my plan would give men encouragement and incentives to share more evenly with women the joys, responsibilities, worries, upsets, and sometimes tedium of raising children from infancy to adulthood. And third, the plan would make quality daycare available from infancy on."[12] How far have we come in achieving those goals?

RBG: We have come a considerable distance. The changes I've seen in my lifetime have been enormous. Of course, we haven't reached nirvana, but the progress we've made makes me hopeful for the future. By the way, I said my affirmative action plan would be for men as teachers in kindergarten and grade schools. I think it would be wonderful for children, if they could see men in caring roles just as they see women.

JR: There was a piece in the *New York Times* recently about how kids who saw toys that defied gender stereotypes were more likely to think that girls should play with trucks and boys with dolls. Is it important to break down stereotypes?

RBG: Yes. *Ms.* magazine had produced recordings of songs for children. One of them was "William's Doll." The song collection is called *Free to Be . . . You and Me.* Marlo Thomas was the prime mover in the venture.

JR: What is your message to the next generation of feminists? What are the goals that remain to be achieved?

RBG: Eliminating unconscious bias. It's powerfully hard to root out. Unconscious bias — well, my favorite illustration is the symphony orchestra. When I was growing up, you never saw a woman in a symphony orchestra except perhaps the harpist. Howard Taubman, a well-known music critic for the *New York Times,* swore he could tell the difference, blindfolded, whether it was a woman or a man playing the piano, or the violin. Someone had the bright idea of putting him to the test. He was blindfolded and what happened? He was all mixed up. He identified a pianist as a man when it was a woman, and he was good enough to admit that unconscious bias was operating. So someone got the even brighter idea to put up a curtain between the people who are auditioning and the judges. And that simple device almost overnight led to women showing up in symphony orchestras in numbers.

Now, I wish we could have a drop curtain in every field of endeavor. One example of the unconscious bias that still exists was a Title VII suit brought in the late seventies. The plaintiffs were women who had not succeeded in getting middle management jobs at AT&T. They did very well on all the standard criteria, but they flunked disproportionately at the last stage. What was that last stage? It was what was called a "total person test." The "total person test" was an executive interviewing the candidate for promotion. And why were women dropping out disproportionately? The executive experienced a certain discomfort in dealing with someone who is different. If he's interviewing a man, well, he sort of knows "this person is just like me," and he's comfortable. But if it's a woman, or a member of a minority group, he feels uncomfortable. This person is a stranger to him, and that shows up in how he rates the candidate.

JR: So the solution to unconscious bias is to bring men and women together?

RBG: Well, the more women — this is something that Justice O'Connor often said, that women of our age should get out there and make a good show, and that will encourage other women, and the more women that are out there doing things, the better off all of us will be.

JR: What remains to be done? You hope that the *Feeney* case, requiring intentional discrimination to prove a constitutional claim of discrimination, should be overturned, and unconscious bias should be recognized as something that should be actionable under the Constitution?

RBG: In a *Feeney*-type case, yes. There should be a claim under the Constitution for the absence of equal treatment. Unconscious bias is hard to combat. The blind symphony orchestra audition is my number one example of the existence of unconscious bias.

JR: How else would the law be transformed if unconscious bias were able to be challenged under the Constitution?

RBG: Many more opportunities would open to women. When it's a one-on-one situation, a woman passed over for promotion, for example, the company will come up with non-gender-related reasons she was not promoted. *Feeney* should have been an easy case because, under the Massachusetts system, you go to the top of the list if you're a veteran. Most veterans' preferences add fifteen points to your score. Under a fifteen-points-added system, many women with top scores could still gain the job or promotion. But when veterans go to the top of the list with a bare pass, women are overwhelmingly excluded.

JR: How about other discrimination suits? Should unconscious racial bias also be actionable?

RBG: Yes, there is no doubt unconscious racial bias. Lilly Ledbetter's case is an example of a certain blindness. The Court said she sued too late. If she had sued early on, Goodyear would have said her low salary had nothing to do with Lilly being a woman — she just didn't do the job as well as the men. Then, year after year, she gets good performance ratings. That defense is no longer available to the company, but she still loses, the Court said, because she sued too late. Congress corrected that error.

JR: What's your message to the new generation of feminists who really look to you as a role model?

RBG: Work for the things that you care about. I think of the seventies. Many young women supported an Equal Rights Amendment. I was a proponent of the ERA. The women of my generation and my daughter's generation were active in moving along the social change that would yield equal citizenship stature for men and women. One thing that concerns me is that some young women today don't seem to care that we have a fundamental instrument of government that makes no express statement about the equal citizenship stature of men and women. They know there are no closed doors anymore, and they may take for granted the rights they have.

JR: We had an extraordinary experience at the Constitution Center: we gave the Liberty Medal to Malala Yousafzai, who's just won the Nobel Peace Prize. And she is the most inspiring seventeen-year-old girl you can imagine. She wrote on her blog, she criticized the Taliban for denying access to education to young women, she survived an assassination attempt, and she has just inspired the world with her advocacy of the importance of education and free speech. Is that the model to follow? Would you encourage young women to be lawyers, to be activists, to be Supreme Court justices — how can they make a difference?

RBG: By not taking no for an answer. If you have a dream, something you want to pursue, and you're willing to do the work that's necessary to make the dream come true, don't let anyone tell you, you can't do it. And you have, nowadays, many like-minded people to join you in opposing unfair treatment, treatment of you as less than a full citizen.

JR: That's, I think, precisely the advice that Malala's father gave her, and that confidence, that with education and hard work you can do anything, is something that's so crucial to success. You've said that you are optimistic about the future because you have hope for the millennials.

RBG: Yes.

JR: Which is wonderful to hear. What is your advice to those young people about how they can best advance the cause of justice?

RBG: Not alone, but in alliance with like-minded people. I was impressed and heartened by the Women's March in DC, which has now been repeated in many places all over the country. Young people should appreciate the values on which our nation is based and how precious they are, and if they don't become part of the crowd that seeks to uphold them — recall something Judge Learned Hand said: if the spirit of liberty dies in the hearts of the people, no court is capable of restoring it. But I can see the spirit of my grandchildren and their friends, and I have faith in this generation just coming into adulthood.

12
MARGARET ATWOOD
MEETS RBG

In the summer of 2018, Justice Ginsburg invited my wife, Lauren, and me to spend the weekend with her and her family at the Glimmerglass opera festival in Cooperstown, New York.

At the top of a hill, we arrived at a Colonial mansion. After a federal marshal showed us to our room, we went downstairs to meet our fellow guests, including the justice's son, Jim Ginsburg, who runs a classical music recording company, and his wife, the soprano and composer Patrice Michaels, who had just recorded *Notorious RBG in Song,* an album for Jim's label, which sets the justice's correspondence and opinions to soaring music.

Justice Ginsburg descended the grand staircase in a blue pantsuit and shawl. She warmly greeted us, and we all piled into an SUV to see a lecture at Glimmerglass by the novelist Margaret Atwood, author of *The*

Handmaid's Tale.

Published in 1985, at the height of the Reagan era, *The Handmaid's Tale* is a dystopian thought experiment about how a theocratic, patriarchal government in the near future might subjugate American women. In her lecture, Atwood said that *The Handmaid's Tale* had recently been adapted as an opera, which would be performed at Glimmerglass soon. And she drew a connection between her book and James Fenimore Cooper, the author of *The Last of the Mohicans,* whose farmhouse in Cooperstown is now the site of the Fenimore Art Museum. In Cooper's time, women wore bonnets to avoid the male gaze, and in *The Handmaid's Tale,* a religious fundamentalist government forces women to wear bonnets to ensure their subordination to their male masters.

In the question-and-answer session with the audience, Atwood said that there had been three explosions of feminism in the twentieth century. The first culminated in the passage of the Nineteenth Amendment, granting women the right to vote. The second feminist explosion, the women's movement of the 1960s and '70s, was a reaction, Atwood said, to the oppression epitomized by life in the 1950s, when suburban women effectively were locked in a house with four kids and no employment prospects. And the third explosion, the #MeToo movement, was a backlash against the harassment women experienced at the hands of predators such as Harvey Weinstein. Atwood said she believed that just as the feminist movement of the 1960s and '70s had provoked the Reagan revolution that led her to imagine *The Handmaid's Tale,* the #MeToo movement would in time provoke a backlash of its own that would set back women's progress and equality.

Atwood had stoked controversy earlier in the year when she criticized the #MeToo movement for failing to protect the due process rights of the accused. In a piece for the Toronto *Globe and Mail* called "Am I a Bad Feminist?," Atwood wrote that she had gotten into trouble with "Good Feminists" two years earlier by defending the due process rights of a creative writing professor accused of sexual misconduct at the University of British Columbia. "The #MeToo moment is a symptom of a broken legal system," Atwood wrote, comparing university sexual misconduct proceedings to "the Salem witchcraft trials, in which a person was guilty because accused, since the rules of evidence were such that you could not be found innocent." Her denunciation of "understandable and temporary vigilante justice" morphing into "a culturally solidified lynch-mob habit"[1] provoked a social media backlash, with one critic accusing "one of the most important feminist voices of our time" of criticizing "less powerful women to uphold the power of her powerful male friend."[2]

Justice Ginsburg, too, had emphasized the need for fairness to the accuser and the accused in college sexual misconduct proceedings. This shared concern made the meeting between the two towering figures especially meaningful. Ginsburg cordially greeted Atwood in the green room after the lecture but expressed more optimism about the future of the #MeToo movement. "Jeff just asked me if I would agree with you that there have been three main stages of feminism in the past century, and I said yes," she told Atwood. "But I don't think there will be a successful backlash this time."

Atwood replied, "I think there will be, and we're already seeing it with Hillary Clinton. I wanted to say in the talk that this is the first time we've seen this seventeenth-century talk of the female witch character."

Ginsburg replied, "I think there are so many women who will come out this time and many women in positions of authority. Women now represent over fifty percent of law school classes and of undergraduates as well. As women are represented in numerical majorities in positions of authority, enough of them will care about their sisters — they will not allow the progress to be reversed."

We walked backstage and then outside the theater, where Justice Ginsburg admired a huge drawing of her that a female stagehand had created in tribute on the pavement. After dinner, during which Atwood joined us to talk with the justice, we took our seats for the evening performance of *West Side Story*. Before the show, the Glimmerglass director announced Justice Ginsburg's presence, and the audience responded with a standing ovation.

The next afternoon, we toured the Fenimore Art Museum, which owns the original letters Alexander Hamilton wrote to Aaron Burr setting up their fatal duel. In the Alexander Hamilton Room, Justice Ginsburg gazed at bronze life masks of John Adams, Thomas Jefferson, the Marquis de Lafayette, and James Madison, and said that although she was about to take her grandchildren to a performance of *Hamilton,* her favorite Founder was Madison.

We walked downstairs to view the museum's collection of Native American art, and Justice Ginsburg paused before two dance fans, created around 1879, from Central Yupik, Alaska, worn on the fingers and used as rattles during ceremonial dances. Next to the fans were two round-faced dance masks surrounded by feathers, one smiling and the other frowning. The smiling face was male, our guide explained, and the frowning face female.

"Is that common, for women to be depicted with frowns and men with smiles?" Justice Ginsburg asked.

"Yes," the guide replied, and the justice's daughter-in-law, Patrice, added, "Why is the eternal question."

That evening, we had dinner again on the grounds of the opera house, before attending the opera *Silent Night,* a musical rendition of a temporary Christmas armistice during World War I. In the spirit of our many informal conversations over the years, Justice Ginsburg invited me to take out my iPhone to record our conversation before dessert. She offered further thoughts about due process and the #MeToo movement, and said that she was "skeptically hopeful" about the future of the Supreme Court in the wake of the retirement of Justice Anthony Kennedy.

JR: If Margaret Atwood was right last night, that we're now in a third feminist movement, what are other legal victories that should follow from it?

RBG: One is giving a woman an opportunity while raising children to have a flexible schedule at work. I was surprised that law firms haven't been as receptive to flextime as they should be, because now an associate has a whole law library at her fingertips. She could work at home, something that wasn't possible in earlier years. A flexible schedule is facilitating for both men and women. We have in DC the first person to be given flexible time at a law firm. It was at Arnold and Porter, and the woman is Brooksley Born. When her second child was born, she elected to have a three-day schedule. She was told, "That's okay, but you'll never make partner." It turned out that she produced more in three days than the average associate produced in a full week, so she became the first full-time [female] partner.

JR: What other legal changes are necessary to secure full equality for women?

262

RBG: The two big areas are unconscious bias and what is called work-life balance. If we could fix those two, we would see women all over doing everything. Unconscious bias and facilitating a work life and a family life.

JR: Are those the goals of the third feminist movement we call #MeToo? If not, what are other goals the movement has?

RBG: I can't speak for young women. I think #MeToo was not possible in an earlier time. One of the women who started it, Ashley Judd, said she gave her story about Harvey Weinstein to the *New York Times* two years — *two years* — before they finally published it. When they did, it had a ripple effect.

JR: Where will this end? What will the legal dimensions of the #MeToo movement be?

RBG: What Margaret Atwood said about #MeToo last night was that you need a structure for making complaints, and you need to build fairness into the system. Many of the women have horrendous stories to tell about their harassment. Then there are cases where the man who is accused doesn't get a fair hearing. Allegations are made, he's assumed to be a bad actor. The person attacked has a right to have his story heard just as the accuser has her story heard. Fairness is an important part of this, fairness to the person who is accused.

JR: And how can we best ensure fairness to the accuser and accused? What kind of process is necessary?

RBG: Well, the ones that have been written into some college codes. Both should have a right to an impartial decider.

JR: Do workplaces also need fair procedures?

RBG: Yes, fair procedures, representation, and an impartial decider. Margaret Atwood spoke about having an independent decision maker from outside the institution.

JR: How would it work? Both workplaces and universities would create separate courts or review boards that would hear the cases?

RBG: Yes, and they might develop something like an arbitration association's procedures, where there's an independent adjudicator.

JR: The important thing is fairness.

RBG: Right.

JR: Based on the experience of the movement of the sixties and seventies, will this movement have a beginning, middle, and end?

RBG: I think of the spirit of my granddaughter and her friends. It reminds me of the spirit among women in the seventies. The backlash, as Margaret said yesterday, too, never takes us all the way back. There are still advances, a way forward, and I do think the more women there are in positions of authority, the less likely that setbacks will occur.

JR: What is the spirit you see in your granddaughter that reminds you of the seventies?

RBG: She wants to end what she sees as injustice to women, and her particular interest is reproductive services for nonaffluent women.

JR: Given the jurisprudence and the likely difficulty of access for poor women in the future, what is the legal solution?

RBG: One route, given the restrictions that legislatures have imposed, is to use state courts and state constitutions, asking courts in certain states to interpret their equal protection clauses the way the Supreme Court might have treated equal protection. It surprised me that after *Roe v. Wade,* when the case concerning Medicaid coverage for abortion came up, the Supreme Court rejected the equality plea. Some state courts might be more sympathetic to the argument that choice means choice for all women, not just women with the means to pay for the services they seek.

JR: If you were a state court writing an equal protection decision along these lines, what would the reasoning be?

RBG: It would be just this: the government is not providing equal protection when Medicaid covers, say, childbirth but not abortion or contraception services.

JR: Would state court decisions along these lines be enough to ensure access to abortion if *Roe* is scaled back or overturned?

RBG: States are not bound to accept for their own constitutions the way the Supreme Court reads the federal constitution.

JR: But the most conservative state courts will reject the reasoning, so poor women will be in worse shape.

RBG: Well, you need a number of states to change. Compare the death penalty. We have fewer and fewer executions each year, in some states because they have changed their laws, in others because they don't enforce their laws. The death penalty may die of attrition. A significant number of states might accept that choice should be for all women, and cease funding one choice but not the other.

JR: So your granddaughter's mission to persuade state courts should really be a cause for other young women because that legal change, state by state, can really make a political difference?

RBG: Yes. First, of course, you try to block restrictive measures by state legislatures. I think it's a healthy thing for a system when there is a dialogue between the legislature and the Court. So if the Court rules one way, as in the Lilly Ledbetter case or *General Electric v. Gilbert* in the seventies, Congress reacts and changes the law.

JR: How do you think Congress and the states might react if *Roe* were overturned, given the strong support for early-term choice throughout the country?

RBG: Many states will never go back to the way it was. And then it will become even more pronounced, to put it bluntly: poor women must breed, affluent women can choose.

JR: Justice Kennedy has retired. Are you now concerned that *Roe* indeed might be overturned?

RBG: *Roe* has pretty strong precedential weight by now. In *Casey,* the issue was squarely before the Court. The Court said no, we will not overrule *Roe.* We have some hopeful examples — the Court refused to overturn *Miranda.* Just last term, in dissent in the sales tax cases, the chief said he thinks those old decisions were wrong, but they have been on the books for years, they survived one reexamination, so we should adhere to them and let the legislature make the change if it so wills. We have no crystal ball, but a second direct confrontation may be ahead. If so, the odds, I think, are in favor of it *not* being successful.

JR: And what about the other big precedents? Affirmative action seems vulnerable.

RBG: It depends upon the area you have in mind. I think in education, you don't need affirmative action for women; they're a majority of university students. One way or another, I think schools will find a way of providing access to minority group members disabled because their education up to the time of university has been well below par. That was brought home to me when I was teaching at Rutgers. In the year of the riots, the school decided to have an aggressive affirmative action program. As one component, any minority student could get one-on-one tutoring by a faculty member. My student scored in the 300s on the LSAT when the top score was 800. He was very bright. No one had ever taught him how to read and write well; it was just that basic. By the end of the year, he was on law review.

JR: Are there any precedents you are concerned about surviving?

RBG: Who knows what will be, what the Court's membership will be? It's no secret that the justice most likely to join the "liberal justices," after Justice O'Connor left us, was Justice Kennedy.

JR: Are you optimistic or pessimistic about the future of the Court now that Justice Kennedy has retired?

RBG: I would say I'm skeptically hopeful.

JR: Very well put. And what makes you skeptically hopeful?

RBG: The hope that the current chief will follow his predecessor, who saved *Miranda* and who wrote the opinion in the *Hibbs* case, the challenge to the Family and Medical Leave Act. It's possible that the current chief will follow that same path. We'll see.

JR: I know how much that *Hibbs* victory meant to you and what a tribute it was to your influence. Why do you think Chief Justice Rehnquist wrote it, and why did he uphold *Miranda*?

RBG: One is a sense of what it means to be chief. In the future, what reputation will be attributed to the Rehnquist Court? What will history's judgment be on the Roberts Court? In Rehnquist's case, it was not just decisions. When he hired Sally Rider to be his administrative assistant — Sally is a lesbian; her partner came with her to various court functions.

JR: You have always had faith in the Court and the law to pursue justice, and you sound, as you said, skeptically hopeful that that may continue. And you would give what message to progressives and liberals who are concerned that the sky may fall?

RBG: As I told you, good precedent built up over years should survive challenge. And how would the chief justice want his court to be perceived when history is told years later.

JR: Was Chief Justice Roberts's vote in the health care case a sign that he cares about the institutional legitimacy of the Court?

RBG: Perhaps. When that decision was announced, the first reporters rushed out and said the health care act has been overturned.

But the chief went on to say, "This is a tax, so it's okay." His opinion on the Commerce Clause and the limits of the Commerce Clause was troubling. If he had come fully on board, saying, "Yes, Congress has the authority under the Commerce Clause, and this is a tax," that would have been just fine. But his going along with a constrained view of the Commerce Clause, in my judgment, is not promising.

JR: As we talk through all these areas, gender equality, affirmative action, I'm feeling — you said skeptically hopeful — I'm feeling reassured. Is there any area that liberals and civil libertarians should be concerned about not getting redress in the courts?

RBG: A big area on which the Court has spoken, decisions I hope will be overturned, relates to money and elections. *Citizens United* is the lead precedent. More and more, we see how huge spending on elections is corrupting our democracy. The same thing holds for partisan gerrymandering. It will be interesting to see what the Court does with that issue next time.

13
THE HEROIC LEGACY

The 2018–19 Supreme Court term was a challenging one for Justice Ginsburg. In November, three months after I saw her at Glimmerglass, she fell in her chambers, fracturing three ribs. The fall proved to be an unexpected blessing: in the course of tests on her broken ribs, doctors found two cancerous growths on her left lung, which, because of the early detection, were successfully removed at the end of December. With remarkable fortitude and determination, Justice Ginsburg continued her work at the Court during her recovery, missing eleven oral arguments for the first time in her twenty-five years on the bench but participating in those cases by reviewing the briefs and transcripts while recuperating at home. At the beginning of February, two weeks before she returned to the bench, Justice Ginsburg made her first public appearance following the surgery at a performance hosted by the National Constitution Center of *Notorious RBG in Song,* a beautiful song cycle, composed and performed by her daughter-in-law Patrice Michaels, which sets Justice Ginsburg's letters and opinions to music. I was thrilled to see the justice after the performance, smiling and strong; it was then that she handed me a note about my mom's recent passing, always thinking of others, even during her own recovery.

This Supreme Court term was the first in which Justice Brett Kavanaugh replaced Justice Anthony Kennedy. It had the highest percentage of five-to-four decisions (28 percent) since the 2012–13 term, 80 percent of which were ideologically split between conservative and liberal justices. The conservative justices prevailed, however, in only 44 percent of the ideologically split five-to-four decisions, as opposed to 100 percent the previous term.[1] With the retirement of Justice Kennedy, Chief Justice John Roberts emerged as the new swing justice, joining the four liberal justices in several crucial cases, including *Madison v. Alabama,* which halted Alabama's effort to execute a mentally ill prisoner, and *Department of Commerce v. New York,* the Trump administration's initial effort to add a citizenship question to the 2020 census. As the first chief justice to serve as the swing vote in close cases since Charles Evans Hughes in the 1930s, Roberts made the Court undeniably his own, joining the four conservative justices in seven five-to-four decisions, most notably *Rucho v. Common Cause,* which held that partisan gerrymandering is a political question beyond the reach of federal courts to regulate. The decision provoked an anguished dissent from Justice Elena Kagan, who criticized the majority's refusal to intervene to ensure "free and fair elections" and quoted the Declaration of Independence's insistence that governments derive "their just Powers from the Consent of the Governed." Her conclusion: "Is that how American democracy is supposed to work?"

Justice Ginsburg wrote six majority opinions, the fewest of any justice during the term. That's partly because she chose to assign an important majority opinion to Justice Kagan in *Gundy v. United States,* where the Court, by a five-to-three vote (Justice Kavanaugh did not participate) refused to resurrect the so-called nondelegation doctrine, which, in the pre–New Deal era, imposed limits on Congress's power to delegate rulemaking authority to administrative agencies. "If [this] delegation is unconstitutional, then most of Government is unconstitutional," Kagan wrote, "dependent as Congress is on the need to give discretion to executive officials to implement its programs." As the most senior justice in three closely divided cases where Chief Justice Roberts and Justice Clarence Thomas were in dissent, Ginsburg also solidified the votes of her newest conservative colleagues by assigning two majority opinions to Justice Neil Gorsuch (who sided with the liberals 20 percent of the time in five-to-four cases), and one to Justice Kavanaugh. Ginsburg had an opportunity to reach out to both justices because of their very different approaches to constitutional interpretation: Gorsuch and Kavanaugh agreed with each other less frequently during their first term than any other two other justices appointed by the same president in the past fifty years. Ginsburg agreed most frequently with Justice Sonia Sotomayor, the only justice to join her dissent from Justice Samuel Alito's opinion in *American Legion v. American Humanist Association,* holding that the state of Maryland could maintain a World War I memorial, the forty-foot Bladensburg peace cross, on public land without violating the First Amendment's prohibition on government establishments of religion.

Despite her convalescence and recovery, Justice Ginsburg wrote her majority opinions more quickly than any other justice, with a record-breaking average time of only seventy-one days between the oral argument and the published decision.[2]

When I arrived in her chambers on July 2, 2019, I marveled at her remarkable powers of focus, which allow her to concentrate entirely on the task at hand, without being distracted by interruptions. (A few months earlier, her clerks had assembled in her chambers for a birthday celebration; when the room was full, she looked up from her desk in surprise, so intently focused on her work that she hadn't noticed the crowd gathering around her.) Soon after the appointed hour she greeted me warmly in the reception room and walked with me into her chambers. There was Brahms chamber music playing in the background — Justice Ginsburg said the performers were the violist Joshua Bell, the pianist Jeremy Denk, and the cellist Steven Isserlis, whom she had invited to play at the Court in May for the justices' spring musicale. We decided to let the beautiful recording, *For the Love of Brahms,* play during the conversation that follows.

JR: We first bonded over music and opera. Why is music so important to you?

RBG: Oh, it's one of the things that makes life beautiful. Even now, most of the time I'm playing something. If I have to, if there's a part of an opinion I just haven't done right, I have to stop listening and start concentrating. Most of the time, I have opera or other beautiful music playing. It's the first thing I do when I get up in the morning, turning on 90.9, which is the classical music station for the DC area. And I have a large supply of my son's CDs. I can't imagine life without music.

JR: Does it take you outside of yourself?

RBG: Yes, opera is great for that. I could be thinking about an opinion or an argument coming up next week, but when I go to the opera, I'm totally immersed in the music, I'm not thinking about briefs or arguments or opinions.

JR: What are some of the opera performances you most remember in your life?

RBG: Cesare Siepi in *Don Giovanni.* He was the ultimate Don. The Met repeated the same production for years and years, so I remember the production Siepi graced very well. He was as suave as they come.

Another was a *Butterfly* I attended in Boston in 1958, when the Met was still traveling. The director, from Japan, taught the women to move like Japanese women. Antoinetta Stella was Cio-Cio-San. There were no fans. It was a very beautiful production.

The Washington Opera opens with *Otello* this year. At the Met some years ago, I attended the last of the *Otello*s they'd been doing for many years — now they have a new one. Thomas Hampson portrayed Iago. He was *great* — the incarnation of evil.

The double debut of Leontyne Price and Franco Corelli in *Trovatore* was perhaps the most grand evening I experienced at the Met.

JR: Wow.

RBG: That debut was at the old Met, as was the *Forza* we attended the night Leonard Warren died. Warren was the finest Rigoletto I ever heard.

JR: Were you there in 1960 when he died?

RBG: Yes, Marty and I were there.

JR: Oh my goodness. Did you realize what happened?

RBG: He finished his great aria, then keeled over. The next person to come on stage was the doctor who tells the baritone that the tenor has survived. The curtain came down and there was a long intermission. When we returned to our seats, Rudolph Bing announced, "Leonard Warren died tonight. The performance will not continue." Richard Tucker was the tenor that night. He and Warren were good friends.

JR: I have to say how stunned I was when, minutes after the term was over, you emailed me that your edits for this manuscript were done. How is your remarkable focus possible? Your discipline and complete dedication to your work — how do you do it?

RBG: I have no magic formula. I've always worked that way. Every time I go over a transcript, I find I was not as articulate as I thought I was. I edit to reduce confusion and add clarity.

JR: You speak in perfect sentences. Your discipline is remarkable. You often share the advice of your mother that emotions like anger and jealousy are unproductive. It's the advice of the great wisdom traditions, but it's extremely hard to achieve in practice.

RBG: Yes.

JR: How do you actually do it?

RBG: Because I realize if I don't get past unproductive emotions, I'll just get bogged down and lose precious time from useful work.

This term was hard for me because, from November when I cracked my ribs to the beginning of May, lung cancer was a major impediment. During that time, the best thing for me was to sit down with an opinion draft, stop thinking about my discomforts, and just do the work.

It was a hard term otherwise, as you've seen the output from the last few weeks of the term. I thought Elena Kagan wrote a wonderful dissent in the partisan gerrymandering case.

JR: She quoted the Declaration of Independence and said the very nature of democracy is at stake. What do you think is at stake with the inability to challenge partisan gerrymandering in the courts?

RBG: Well, there's still some hope in the state courts. Pennsylvania is one state that held extreme gerrymandering incompatible with the state's constitution. There's slim possibility of change here, given the current composition of the Court.

And then, I was sad, although I expected it, that only one colleague, Justice Sotomayor, joined me in the Bladensburg cross case. Breyer's comment: perhaps our division reflected the difference between growing up in San Francisco, as he did, and growing up in Brooklyn, as I did.

JR: There must have been crosses there, too. You had a lone friend in Justice Gorsuch in the double jeopardy case.

RBG: Yes. In fact, people who pay close attention to what we do will have noticed I assigned two opinions to Gorsuch this term and one to Kavanaugh. I was the assigning justice because the chief and Justice Thomas were on the other side, leaving me the most senior justice in the majority.

JR: What did you make of Justice Kavanaugh's first term?

RBG: He's very congenial, he works very hard, and he's responsible for a very important first: all of his law clerks are women. The result, for the first time in history more women than men served as law clerks at the Court.

JR: And how about Justice Gorsuch?

RBG: He's also very congenial. But on some issues, one can predict his view. That, I suppose, is true of all of us. An important case this term, *Gundy,* concerned the revival of the nondelegation doctrine. This issue will come back, I think sooner rather than later, when there are nine justices participating.

JR: In *Gundy,* Justice Kagan's majority opinion said this would mean the end of government. Is that what would happen if the nondelegation doctrine were revived?

RBG: Well, we will have to see. The doctrine hasn't figured in the Court's jurisprudence since the early New Deal Court.

JR: What are the stakes for the Court? Help people understand why the revival of the nondelegation doctrine, all these doctrines that make it hard for government to function, would make such a huge difference.

RBG: It's hard for people to understand the field of administrative law. Of course, there is a check against agency abuse of authority. Congress can give an agency broad discretion, but, if Congress doesn't like what the agency has done, Congress can stop it. I don't understand the view that the legislature has to spell out in a statute what it really can't foresee.

JR: In such a polarized time, in practice, does it make government very difficult, if Congress has to spell everything out?

RBG: I don't know how we get Congress to start working again. But I remain optimistic when I see my granddaughter and her friends. Clara knows the importance of getting people to vote.

JR: How has the Court changed now that Justice Kavanaugh has replaced Justice Kennedy?

RBG: I think the big change came when Sandra left. She left us in the middle of the term. In the months she was absent, in all the closely divided cases, I would have been in the majority rather than the minority had she stayed.

Did you read Evan Thomas's biography [of Justice O'Connor]? It's very well done. One correction. Thomas describes how I scraped her car while parking in the Court's garage. Someone in Phoenix exaggerated that story. Evan Thomas, in an attempt to explain my bad driving, said I didn't learn to drive until I was middle-aged, when we moved to DC. In fact, I got my driver's license when I was twenty! It's true I was a very bad driver, but scraping Sandra's car happened only once, not multiple times.

[Laughter.]

JR: Next year is the one hundredth anniversary of the Nineteenth Amendment. Might the Equal Rights Amendment be revived? Is there some chance of it?

RBG: Yes, I think there is. But I'd like to see it start anew. There's a thought that the ERA will succeed if three more states ratify, but I don't think you can play the game that way, because a number of states have withdrawn their ratification, so you'd have to count those. It would be better to start over. I hope that that will happen.

JR: If you were making the case for why it's important to ratify the ERA now, what would you say?

RBG: Equal citizenship stature for men and women belongs in any fundamental instrument of government. It should be as basic to society as free speech and freedom of religion. And it is stated among basic rights in every post-1950 constitution in the world. Many countries honor it in the breach, but it is at least recognized as basic to human rights. There's a certain irony in using the Equal Protection Clause to ensure the equal citizenship stature of men and women. The Clause appears in an amendment that, for the first time, introduced the word "male" into the Constitution.

JR: This is why you're not an originalist?

RBG: I am an originalist; I think we're constantly forming a more perfect Union, which is what the Founders intended. As bad as things may be, they are better than they once were. These are not the best of times, but think of how many bad times I've experienced in my long life. Starting with the Second World War, overwhelming when I was growing up. Then Senator Joe McCarthy when I was in college. Then Vietnam. Somehow, we have gotten over the worst of times.

JR: And the Constitution, as you put it, has become ever more embracive. That's such a beautiful word, and it's your word. What do you mean by embracive?

RBG: Embracing the left-out people as part of the community, not grudgingly, but with open arms.

JR: And for you, that's what the Constitution should do?

RBG: Yes, I believe that is what the Founders anticipated.

JR: I saw a 2010 poll suggesting that more Americans support originalism than living constitutionalism, 49 percent versus 42 percent. Why do you think that's the case?

RBG: Because I don't think there's a clear understanding of what either term means.

JR: So, help us understand. What does the original Constitution mean?

RBG: The original Constitution, as amended by the Bill of Rights, includes many themes that would apply to society as it evolves over time, freedom of speech, press, and religion, and due process of law, most notably. And equality imbued the Declaration of Independence although the stain of slavery kept that ideal out of the Constitution until 1868.

JR: And you believe it's important to extend the protections of the Constitution in order to fulfill its promise, and the promise of the Declaration?

RBG: The Declaration is our first statement of the idea of equality, though that great statement, "all [persons] are created equal," was penned by a slave owner.

JR: I reread the essay you wrote at the age

of thirteen about the Declaration, the Magna Carta, the Ten Commandments, and the United Nations Charter. It made me weep.

RBG: Well, that was a very hopeful time. People dreamed of one world and President Franklin Delano Roosevelt's Four Freedoms. I'm going to a New York University conference in Lisbon that starts out with a set of writings about Brexit. Next topic, the disintegration of democracy.

JR: This theme of the rise of populism around the West is crucial. Are you concerned that we're seeing the rise of the kind of demagogues the Founders feared?

RBG: Yes.

JR: Social media is part of that?

RBG: Yes, and an important part is the discontent seen among people who feel that our institutions of government pay no attention to them, as illustrated by J. D. Vance's *Hillbilly Elegy.*

JR: Fixing democracy is a task bigger than any of us. But what are some things that could be done?

RBG: One key thing is to teach children about democracy. They don't learn about it in school as they did in civics classes when I was young. By the way, did you see the show *What the Constitution Means to Me*?

JR: Not yet, but I know you did see it. What did you think?

RBG: I loved it. At the end of the second act, a teenager comes on stage to take part in the conversation about the Constitution. Two young women alternate in that role. The older one, age eighteen, played the role the night I attended. She just graduated from high school, and I will stay in touch with her. I was uplifted by those young women.

JR: What is uplifting about them? What's the message of the play?

RBG: The play begins with a young woman who wins American Legion competitions, by spouting rosy things about the Constitution. Then, she questions whether the Constitution is as protective as she portrayed it in her youth. At the end, she puts the question to the audience: Should we keep it or should we do it over? Our audience voted overwhelmingly to keep it, and it's been overwhelmingly that way for most audiences.

JR: Why are people moved to keep it? And why should we keep it?

RBG: What reason is there to think we would do better if we started over from scratch?

JR: Thank you so much for what you wrote about my mom. And what you said about carrying on in your life and work is the crucial thing.

RBG: She sounds like someone I would have liked.

JR: If you had to give advice to young girls or boys about how to muster the self-discipline and focus to lead productive and empathetic lives, what would it be?

RBG: If you want your dreams to come true, you must be willing to put in the hard work it takes to make that possible. We live in a society where, with will, determination, and dedication, you can be whatever you have the talent to be. I would also advise that good citizens have obligations as well as rights, the obligation to help keep our democracy relevant. Young people should pursue something outside themselves, something they are passionate about: ending discrimination or keeping our planet safe, for example.

JR: Are you optimistic or pessimistic about the future of the Court?

RBG: I revere the Court. I think all of the justices do. More than anything else, we want to make sure we leave it as healthy as we found it. For the most part, the U.S. Supreme Court has been exemplary, not only a model for our own country, but for the world, a model of the independence of the judiciary and of the obligation to reason why. Unlike the political branches of government, we must give reasons for our opinions. Hope springs eternal. I try to be as persuasive as I can in conference and in writing opinions. Sometimes I'm successful, sometimes not. But I will continue to try.

NOTES

The conversations included in this book were drawn from the following interviews conducted by the author:

"A Conversation with Justice Ruth Bader Ginsburg," Aspen Ideas Festival, Aspen, Colorado, July 8, 2010.

"An Evening with Justice Ruth Bader Ginsburg," National Constitution Center, Philadelphia, Pennsylvania, September 6, 2013.

Interview with Justice Ruth Bader Ginsburg after the National Constitution Center performance of *Scalia/Ginsburg*, Washington, DC, April 24, 2014.

"Ruth Bader Ginsburg Is an American Hero," *New Republic*, September 28, 2014.

"A Conversation with Supreme Court Justice Ruth Bader Ginsburg," The Aspen Institute, Washington, DC, October 27, 2014.

"A Conversation with Justice Ruth Bader

Ginsburg," National Constitution Center, Philadelphia, Pennsylvania, February 12, 2018.

Interview with Justice Ruth Bader Ginsburg at Glimmerglass, Cooperstown, New York, August 18, 2018.

Interview with Justice Ruth Bader Ginsburg at the Supreme Court, Washington, DC, July 2, 2019.

Introduction

Cases cited, listed in order in which they appear in the text.

Welsh v. United States, 398 U.S. 333 (1970)

Moritz v. Commissioner, 469 F.2d 466 (10th Cir. 1972)

Roe v. Wade, 410 U.S. 113 (1973)

Ibanez v. Florida Department of Business and Professional Regulation, Board of Accountancy, 512 U.S. 136 (1994)

Ratzlaf v. United States, 510 U.S. 135 (1994)

Bush v. Gore, 531 U.S. 98 (2000)

1. Ruth Bader Ginsburg, "Some Thoughts on Judicial Authority to Repair Unconstitutional Legislation," *Cleveland State Law Review* 28 (1979): 301, http://engaged scholarship.csuohio.edu/clevstlrev/vol28/iss3/3.

2. Jeffrey Rosen, "The List," *New Republic,* May 10, 1993, https://newrepublic.com/

article/73769/the-list-0.

3. Daniel Patrick Moynihan to Martin Peretz, April 10, 1994. On file with author.
4. Suzy Hagstrom, "Silvia Safille Ibanez, Still Fighting After a Big Victory," *Orlando Sentinel,* December 31, 1995, http://articles.orlandosentinel.com/1995-12-31/news/9512291309_1_ibanez-florida-certified-financial.
5. Jeffrey Rosen, "The New Look of Liberalism on the Court," *New York Times Magazine,* October 5, 1997, https://archive.nytimes.com/www.nytimes.com/library/politics/scotus/articles/100597nytmag-ginsburg-profile.html.

Chapter 1: Her Landmark Cases
Cases cited:
Brown v. Board of Education of Topeka, 347 U.S. 483 (1954)
Hoyt v. Florida, 368 U.S. 57 (1961)
Reed v. Reed, 404 U.S. 71 (1971)
Frontiero v. Richardson, 411 U.S. 677 (1973)
Welsh v. United States, 398 U.S. 333 (1970)
Craig v. Boren, 429 U.S. 190 (1976)
Weinberger v. Wiesenfeld, 420 U.S. 636 (1975)
Goesaert v. Cleary, 335 U.S. 464 (1948)

1. "Reed vs. Reed at 40: Equal Protection and Women's Rights," *Journal of Gender,*

Chapter 2: Marriage Between Equals

1. Jane Sherron De Hart, *Ruth Bader Ginsburg: A Life* (New York: Alfred A. Knopf, 2018), p. 44.
2. Ibid., p. 56.
3. Ruth Bader Ginsburg, "The Status of Women: Introduction," *American Journal of Comparative Law* 20 (1972): 509–25.
4. Martin D. Ginsburg, "Reflections on Supreme Court Spousehood," delivered at Ninth Circuit Judicial Conference Breakfast, Maui, Hawaii, August 22, 1995.
5. De Hart, *Ruth Bader Ginsburg,* p. 416.
6. Hanna Rosin, "The End of Men," *Atlantic* (July/August 2010), https://www.theatlantic.com/magazine/archive/2010/07/the-end-of-men/308135/.

Chapter 3: *Roe*

Cases cited:
Roe v. Wade, 410 U.S. 113 (1973)
Planned Parenthood of Southeastern Pennsylvania v. Casey, 505 U.S. 833 (1992)
Struck v. Secretary of Defense, 409 U.S. 1071 (1972)
Gonzales v. Carhart, 550 U.S. 124 (2007)
Stenberg v. Carhart, 530 U.S. 914 (2000)

McCullen v. Coakley, 573 U.S. 464 (2014)

1. Ruth Bader Ginsburg, "Speaking in a Judicial Voice," Madison Lecture Series, *New York University Law Review* 67 (1992): 1199.
2. Ibid., p. 1208.
3. Ruth Bader Ginsburg, "Some Thoughts on Autonomy and Equality in Relation to *Roe v. Wade*," *North Carolina Law Review,* vol. 53 (1985): 385.
4. Ginsburg, "Speaking in a Judicial Voice," p. 1198.

Chapter 4: The Bill of Rights and Equal Protection

Cases cited:

United States v. Virginia, 518 U.S. 515 (1996)

M.L.B. v. S.L.J., 519 U.S. 102 (1996)

Olsen v. Drug Enforcement Administration, 878 F.2d 1458 (D.C. Cir. 1989)

Burwell v. Hobby Lobby Stores, Inc., 573 U.S. 682 (2014)

Young v. United Parcel Service, Inc., 575 U.S. _____ (2015)

Geduldig v. Aiello, 417 U.S. 484 (1974)

General Electric Co. v. Gilbert, 429 U.S. 125 (1976)

Welsh v. United States, 398 U.S. 333 (1970)

California Federal Savings & Loan Associa-

tion v. Guerra, 479 U.S. 272 (1987)

Vorchheimer v. School District of Philadelphia, 400 F. Supp. 326 (E.D. Pa. 1975)

Smith v. Doe, 538 U.S. 84 (2003)

Gideon v. Wainwright, 372 U.S. 335 (1963)

Snyder v. Phelps, 131 S. Ct. 1207 (2011)

Riley v. California, 573 U.S. _____ (2014)

United States v. Jones, 565 U.S. 400 (2012)

1. De Hart, *Ruth Bader Ginsburg,* p. 35.
2. *Vorchheimer v. School District of Philadelphia,* 400 F. Supp. 326 (E.D. Pa. 1975).
3. *M.L.B. v. S.L.J.,* 519 U.S. 102 (1996).
4. *Olson v. Drug Enforcement Administration,* 878 F.2d 1458 (D.C. Cir. 1989).
5. *Young v. United Parcel Service, Inc.,* 575 U.S. _____ (2015).
6. *Geduldig v. Aiello,* 417 U.S. 484, 496 n.20 (1974).
7. Ruth Bader Ginsburg and Susan Deller Ross, "Pregnancy and Discrimination," *New York Times,* January 25, 1977, https://www.nytimes.com/1977/01/25/archives/pregnancy-and-discrimination.html.
8. Ruth Bader Ginsburg, "Some Thoughts on the 1980's Debate over Special versus Equal Treatment for Women," *Law & Inequality* 4 (1986): 145, http://scholarship.law.umn.edu/lawineq/vol4/iss1/11.

Chapter 5: Sisters in Law

Cases cited:

Safford Unified School District v. Redding, 557 U.S. 364 (2009)

Bush v. Gore, 531 U.S. 98 (2000)

United States v. Virginia, 518 U.S. 515 (1996)

Citizens United v. Federal Election Commission, 558 U.S. 310 (2010)

Shelby County v. Holder, 570 U.S. 529 (2013)

Burwell v. Hobby Lobby Stores, Inc., 573 U.S. 682 (2014)

1. Ruth Bader Ginsburg, "The Progression of Women in the Law," *Valparaiso Law Review* 29 (1994): 1175.
2. Ibid., p. 1174.
3. De Hart, *Ruth Bader Ginsburg,* p. 383.
4. Ibid.
5. Transcript of Oral Argument in *Safford Unified School District No. 1 v. Redding,* 45–46, April 21, 2009, https://www.supremecourt.gov/oral_arguments/argument_transcripts/2008/08-479.pdf.
6. *Safford Unified School District No. 1 v. Redding,* 557 U.S. 364 (2009) (Ginsburg, J., concurring).
7. De Hart, *Ruth Bader Ginsburg,* p. 328.
8. Remarks by Justice Ruth Bader Ginsburg on Presentation of Torchbearer Award to

Justice Sandra Day O'Connor, Women's Bar Association of Washington, DC, May 14, 1997.

9. Joan Biskupic, "Female Justices Attest to Fraternity on the Bench," *Washington Post,* August 21, 1994, https://www .washingtonpost.com/archive/politics/ 1994/08/21/female-justices-attest-to -fraternity-on-bench/b43a9c49-8b7b-4adc -9972-ceb31402287a/?utm_term=.12bae 40d0b9c.

10. Remarks by Justice Ginsburg, Presentation of Torchbearer Award.

11. "When Will There Be Enough Women on the Supreme Court? Justice Ginsburg Answers That Question," *PBS NewsHour,* PBS, February 5, 2015, https://www.pbs .org/newshour/show/justice-ginsburg -enough-women-supreme-court.

12. De Hart, *Ruth Bader Ginsburg,* p. 382.

13. Ibid., p. 341.

14. Ruth Bader Ginsburg, foreword to Bryant Johnson, *The RBG Workout: How She Stays Strong . . . and You Can Too!* (New York: Houghton Mifflin Harcourt, 2017), p. 6.

15. Carla Herreria, "Ruth Bader Ginsburg Slams Senate Hearings as a 'Highly Partisan Show,' " *Huffington Post,* September 13, 2018, https://www.huffingtonpost

.com/entry/ruth-bader-ginsburg-senate
-supreme-court-hearings_us_5b999d0fe
4b0162f4733cf91.

Chapter 6: Nino
Cases cited:
Bush v. Gore, 531 U.S. 98 (2000)
District of Columbia v. Heller, 554 U.S. 570 (2008)
Craig v. Boren, 429 U.S. 190 (1976)
Gonzales v. Carhart, 550 U.S. 124 (2007)
Maryland v. King, 569 U.S. 435 (2013)

1. Rosen, "The List"; Ruth Bader Ginsburg, Eulogy for Justice Antonin Scalia, March 1, 2016, https://awpc.cattcenter.iastate .edu/2017/03/21/eulogy-for-justice -antonin-scalia-march-1-2016.
2. "The Case of the Notorious RBG: New at Reason," *Reason,* January 5, 2019, https://reason.com/blog/2019/01/05/the -case-of-the-notorious-rbg-new-at-rea.
3. "Supreme Court Justices Weigh In on Antonin Scalia's Death," *USA Today,* February 14, 2016, https://www.usatoday.com/ story/news/politics/2016/02/14/statements -supreme-court-death-justice-scalia/ 80375976/./.
4. Ginsburg, Eulogy for Justice Antonin Scalia.
5. Herreria, "Ruth Bader Ginsburg Slams

301

Senate Hearings."

6. Christopher E. Smith et al., "The First-Term Performance of Ruth Bader Ginsburg," *Judicature* 78 (1994–95): 74, https://heinonline.org/HOL/LandingPage?handle=hein.journals/judica78&div=21&id=&page=.

7. Ginsburg, Eulogy for Justice Antonin Scalia.

8. Joan Biskupic, *The Chief: The Life and Turbulent Times of Chief Justice John Roberts* (New York: Basic Books, 2019), p. 306.

Chapter 7: The Two Chiefs

Cases cited:

Frontiero v. Richardson, 411 U.S. 677 (1973)

Taylor v. Louisiana, 419 U.S. 522 (1975)

United States v. Morrison, 529 U.S. 598 (2000)

Nevada Department of Human Resources v. Hibbs, 538 U.S. 721 (2003)

United States v. Virginia, 518 U.S. 515 (1996)

Citizens United v. Federal Election Commission, 558 U.S. 310 (2010)

Shelby County v. Holder, 570 U.S. 529 (2013)

National Federation of Independent Business v. Sebelius, 567 U.S. 519 (2012)

Miranda v. Arizona, 384 U.S. 436 (1966)
Burwell v. Hobby Lobby Stores, Inc., 573 U.S. 682 (2014)

1. Ruth Bader Ginsburg, "In Memoriam: William H. Rehnquist," *Harvard Law Review,* vol. 119 (2005): 6.
2. De Hart, *Ruth Bader Ginsburg,* p. 327.
3. Jeffrey Rosen, "Rehnquist the Great?," *Atlantic,* April 2005, https://www.theatlantic.com/magazine/archive/2005/04/rehnquist-the-great/303820/.
4. Bernard Weinraub, "Burger Retiring, Rehnquist Named Chief; Scalia, Appeals Judge, Chosen for Court," *New York Times,* June 18, 1986, https://www.nytimes.com/1986/06/18/us/burger-retiring-rehnquist-named-chief-scalia-appeals-judge-chosen-for-court.html.

Chapter 8: When a Dissent Sparked a Meme

Cases cited:
Shelby County v. Holder, 570 U.S. 529 (2013)
Burwell v. Hobby Lobby Stores, Inc., 573 U.S. 682 (2014)
Gonzales v. Carhart, 550 U.S. 124 (2007)
Ledbetter v. Goodyear Tire & Rubber Co., 550 U.S. 618 (2007)
National Federation of Independent Business

v. Sebelius, 567 U.S. 519 (2012)

Trump v. Hawaii, 585 U.S. (2018)

Masterpiece Cakeshop, Ltd. v. Colorado Civil Rights Commission, 584 U.S. (2018)

Bush v. Gore, 531 U.S. 98 (2000)

Northwest Austin Municipal Utility District No. 1 v. Holder, 557 U.S. 193 (2009)

Roe v. Wade, 410 U.S. 113 (1973)

Dred Scott v. Sandford, 60 U.S. 393 (1857)

Plessy v. Ferguson, 163 U.S. 537 (1896)

1. Ruth Bader Ginsburg, "Dinner Remarks," Embassy of the United States, Madrid, July 23, 1996.

2. *Notorious R.B.G.* (blog), Tumblr, June 25, 2013, entry, http://notoriousrbg.tumblr.com/post/53878784482/throwing-out-preclearance-when-it-has-worked-and.

3. Saba Hamedy, "The Authors of 'Notorious RBG' on Why They First Started a Tumblr About Ruth Bader Ginsburg," *Los Angeles Times,* January 25, 2015, https://www.latimes.com/books/reviews/la-ca-jc-notorious-rbg-20151025-story.html.

4. Ibid.

5. *Burwell v. Hobby Lobby Stores, Inc.,* 573 U.S. 682 (2014) (Ginsburg, J., dissenting).

6. Ruth Bader Ginsburg, "Styles of Collegial Judging: One Judge's Perspective,"

Federal Bar News and Journal 39 (1992): 200.

7. Ruth Bader Ginsburg, "Remarks on Writing Separately," *Washington Law Review* 65 (1990): 133.
8. Ginsburg, "Speaking in a Judicial Voice," p. 1192.
9. Ruth Bader Ginsburg, "Interpretations of the Equal Protection Clause," *Harvard Journal of Law and Public Policy,* vol. 9 (1986): 41.
10. Ginsburg, "Speaking in a Judicial Voice," p. 1193.
11. *Notorious R.B.G.*

Chapter 9: The Cases She Would Overturn
Cases cited:

Fisher v. University of Texas at Austin, 579 U.S. _____ (2016)
United States v. Carolene Products Co., 304 U.S. 144 (1938)
Citizens United v. Federal Election Commission, 558 U.S. 310 (2010)
Gonzales v. Carhart, 550 U.S. 124 (2007)
United States v. Windsor, 570 U.S. 744 (2013)
Hollingsworth v. Perry, 570 U.S. 693 (2013)
Maher v. Roe, 432 U.S. 464 (1977)
Harris v. McRae, 448 U.S. 297 (1980)
National Federation of Independent Business

v. Sebelius, 567 U.S. 519 (2012)

Shelby County v. Holder, 570 U.S. 529 (2013)

Korematsu v. United States, 323 U.S. 214 (1944)

Lochner v. New York, 198 U.S. 45 (1905)

Bowers v. Hardwick, 478 U.S. 186 (1986)

Lawrence v. Texas, 539 U.S. 558 (2003)

United States v. Virginia, 518 U.S. 515 (1996)

Roe v. Wade, 410 U.S. 113 (1973)

Chapter 10: Measured Motions

Cases cited:

Roe v. Wade, 410 U.S. 113 (1973)

Brown v. Board of Education of Topeka, 347 U.S. 483 (1954)

Loving v. Virginia, 388 U.S. 1 (1967)

Skilling v. U.S. 561 U.S. 358 (2010)

Citizens United v. Federal Election Commission, 558 U.S. 310 (2010)

Chevron U.S.A., Inc. v. NRDC, 467 U.S. 837 (1984)

Dred Scott v. Sandford, 60 U.S. 393 (1857)

Plessy v. Ferguson, 163 U.S. 537 (1896)

Furman v. Georgia, 408 U.S. 238 (1972)

Gregg v. Georgia, 428 U.S. 153 (1976)

1. Ginsburg, "Speaking in a Judicial Voice," p. 1208.
2. Ibid., p. 1206.

3. Ibid., p. 1207.
4. Ruth Bader Ginsburg, "Inviting Judicial Activism: A 'Liberal' or 'Conservative' Technique?," *Georgia Law Review* 15 (1981): 542.
5. Ibid., p. 544.
6. Ibid., p. 545.
7. Jeffrey Rosen, "Supreme Court, Inc.," *New York Times Magazine,* March 16, 2008, https://www.nytimes.com/2008/03/16/magazine/16supreme-t.html.
8. *Riegel v. Medtronics,* 552 U.S. 312 (2008).
9. *Gutierrez-Brizuela v. Lynch,* 834 F.3d 1142 (10th Cir., 2016).
10. Ginsburg, "Inviting Judicial Activism," p. 553.
11. Thomas M. Keck, *The Most Activist Supreme Court in History: The Road to Modern Judicial Conservatism* (Chicago: University of Chicago Press, 2004), p. 251.

Chapter 11: #MeToo and a More Perfect Union

Cases cited:

Marschall v. Land Nordrhein-Westfalen, Case No.C-409/95, (1997) ECR I-6363
Regents of University of California v. Bakke, 438 U.S. 265 (1978)
Personnel Administrator of Massachusetts v.

Feeney, 442 U.S. 256 (1979)

Ledbetter v. Goodyear Tire & Rubber Co., 550 U.S. 618 (2007)

1. Ruth Bader Ginsburg, "Women's Right to Full Participation in Shaping Society's Course: An Evolving Constitutional Precept," in Betty Justice and Renate Pore, *Toward the Second Decade: The Impact of the Women's Movement on American Institutions* (Westport, CT: Greenwood Press, 1981), p. 174.

2. Ibid., p. 175.

3. Ibid., p. 174.

4. Catharine A. MacKinnon, *Feminism Unmodified: Discourses on Life and Law* (Cambridge, MA: Harvard University Press, 1987), p. 35.

5. Jeffrey Rosen, "The Book of Ruth," *New Republic,* August 2, 1993.

6. Ginsburg, "Some Thoughts on the 1980's Debate."

7. Ibid., p. 150.

8. Ruth Bader Ginsburg, "Some Thoughts on Benign Classification in the Context of Sex," *Connecticut Law Review* 10 (1978): 825, citing *Leisner v. New York Telephone Co.,* 358 F. Supp. 359 (S.D.N.Y. 1973).

9. Ruth Bader Ginsburg and Deborah Jones Merritt, "Affirmative Action: An International Human Rights Dialogue," *Cardozo*

Law Review 21 (1999): 279.

10. Ginsburg, "Women's Right to Full Participation," p. 187.
11. Ginsburg, "Some Thoughts on the 1980's Debate," p. 150.
12. Ibid., p. 146.

Chapter 12: Margaret Atwood Meets RBG

Cases cited:

Roe v. Wade, 410 U.S. 113 (1973)

Ledbetter v. Goodyear Tire & Rubber Co., 550 U.S. 618 (2007)

General Electric Co. v. Gilbert, 429 U.S. 125 (1976)

Planned Parenthood of Southeastern Pennsylvania v. Casey, 505 U.S. 833 (1992)

Miranda v. Arizona, 384 U.S. 436 (1966)

Nevada Department of Human Resources v. Hibbs, 538 U.S. 721 (2003)

Citizens United v. Federal Election Commission, 558 U.S. 310 (2010)

1. Margaret Atwood, "Am I a Bad Feminist?," *Globe and Mail* (Toronto), January 15, 2018, https://www.theglobeandmail .com/opinion/am-i-a-bad-feminist/arti cle37591823/./.
2. Ashifa Kassam, "Margaret Atwood Faces Feminist Backlash on Social Media over #MeToo," *Guardian,* January 15, 2018, https://www.theguardian.com/books/2018/

jan/15/margaret-atwood-feminist-backlash
-metoo.

Chapter 13: The Heroic Legacy

Cases cited:

Madison v. Alabama, 586 U.S. _____
(2019)

Department of Commerce v. New York, 586
U.S. _____ (2019)

Rucho v. Common Cause, 588 U.S. _____
(2019)

American Legion v. American Humanist Assn.,
588 U.S. _____ (2019)

Gundy v. United States, 588 U.S.
_____ (2019)

1. Adam Feldman, "Final Stat Pack for October Term 2018," SCOTUSblog (June 28, 2019), https://www.scotusblog.com/2019/06/final-stat-pack-for-october-term-2018/.

2. Ibid.

ACKNOWLEDGMENTS

Estelle Rosen, my beloved mother, passed away on January 27, 2019. A week later, Justice Ginsburg gave me the handwritten note quoted in the dedication. Justice Ginsburg was correct about my mother's determination to thrive in the challenges and joys of being alive.

Estelle Rosen was a force of nature. She communed with nature — impressing everyone she met, ever since she was a child, with her remarkable ability to name birds, mushrooms, plants, and flowers. And she forcefully embodied the force of nature through her large personality — her enthusiasm for life, her instance on cultivating her own individuality through music, reading, singing, and dance, and her passion for lifelong learning, which inspired her family, and everyone she met, to be passionate lifelong learners as well.

Like Justice Ginsburg, Mom was born in

Brooklyn in 1933, a month after the justice. At the turn of the last century, her mother, Bertha Wolinsky Katzenberg, and her father, Joseph Katzenberg, accompanied by their families, fled the pogroms in Ekaterinoslav and Bessarabia and set out for America and freedom, arriving as young children at Ellis Island in New York City. Mom grew up in the Bronx, where she thrived in public schools near the New York Botanical Garden and the Bronx Zoo. In high school, Mom won a prize for best student of English and her ambition, according to her high school yearbook, was to dance with Martha Graham, the Picasso of modern dance. She fulfilled that ambition the following year by taking the subway from City College in Harlem to study at Graham's small studio on Broadway. From Graham and her immigrant parents, Mom absorbed the values that she would pass along to her children: the importance of passionate enthusiasm for books and music, and of focused self-discipline and practice that allows each of us to express our unique vitality and individuality.

After City College, where she studied English and anthropology, she went on to the Columbia School of Social Work, where she developed a specialty in family therapy.

An accomplished family therapist, she worked for more than six decades in private practice and at the Jewish Board of Family and Children's Services, where she taught and supervised other family therapists. Her counseling and teaching had a great impact on the lives of others. She was married for fifty-six years to my father, Dr. Sidney Rosen, and they lived together in New York City and in Saugerties, New York, where she communed with the nature she adored. Her enthusiasm for life and her powerful determination to cultivate her own faculties of reason and passion were among her many gifts to her adoring family.

Mom was as excited as I was when Justice Ginsburg agreed to support the writing and publication of this book, and I am grateful beyond words to the justice for taking the time to review the manuscript. Justice Ginsburg is an inspiration on so many levels, including how to live a good life — a life of disciplined focus and self-mastery, dedicated to the welfare of others. Justice Ginsburg exemplifies this inspiring self-mastery, warmth, and concern for others in everything she does, including during our exchanges about this project. She is a remarkably attentive copy editor and deadline enforcer, and her clarity and speed in making her wishes clear, as well as her determination to use every moment of the day for productive work or elevating music and leisure, inspire me every day, as I hope they will inspire readers. Thanks to her efforts as a pathbreaking advocate, judge, and Supreme Court justice, "The idea of 'We the People,' " as she puts it, "has become more and more embracive." She is a personal and constitutional hero.

I'm fortunate, for the third time, to have written a short book on a tight deadline with the help of Paul Golob, a great editor and good friend. Paul conceived of this book as a series of conversations organized around common themes and sharpened it, as always, with his deft trimming, keen requests for clarifications, and kindly but firm deadline enforcement. Thanks also to Paul's assistant Fiora Elbers-Tibbitts, for helping us move the manuscript swiftly through production and to my agent, Rafe Sagalyn, for helping me shape the book in conversations with Paul. At the National Constitution Center, my colleague Lana Ulrich, director of constitutional content, helped me prepare the transcripts, proofread the manuscript, and check all the footnotes. I'm grateful to her, and to all of my wonderful colleagues at the NCC. They make me feel lucky to go to work every day in our common mission to inspire Americans of all ages to learn more about the U.S. Constitution, which Justice Ginsburg has done so much to shape.

Sidney Rosen, my wise and kind dad, a psychiatrist, guru, and sage to so many patients, turned ninety-three and finished his own book as I was completing this one. Working with him on the introductions to his dazzling manuscript, *Understanding Ericksonian Hypnotherapy: The Selected Writings of Sidney Rosen,* taught me so much about the power of the imagination to transform reality. My cherished sons, Hugo and Sebastian Rosen, continue to inspire as they cultivate their minds, bodies, and faculties, immersing themselves in music, sports, reading, and vigorous debates.

My beloved wife, Lauren Coyle Rosen, read every word of the manuscript and greatly improved its structure, nuance, and flow. I am dazzled every day by her brilliance and creativity and so grateful for the opportunity to learn with her, devoting our shared moments of leisure to reading or listening to music together, and to spiritual and intellectual growth.

ABOUT THE AUTHOR

Jeffrey Rosen is the author of six books, most recently *Louis D. Brandeis* and *William Howard Taft*. He is the president and chief executive officer of the National Constitution Center, a law professor at George Washington University, and a contributing writer for *The Atlantic*. He was previously the legal affairs editor of *The New Republic* and a staff writer for *The New Yorker*.

The employees of Thorndike Press hope you have enjoyed this Large Print book. All our Thorndike, Wheeler, and Kennebec Large Print titles are designed for easy reading, and all our books are made to last. Other Thorndike Press Large Print books are available at your library, through selected bookstores, or directly from us.

For information about titles, please call:
(800) 223-1244

or visit our website at:
gale.com/thorndike

To share your comments, please write:
Publisher
Thorndike Press
10 Water St., Suite 310
Waterville, ME 04901